Praise for *Talking with the Tarot*

"Forget stiff, textbook tarot! In this delightful book, Samantha Rose Hicks shows you how to chat with your deck like an old friend—an approach that makes tarot feel fun, accessible, and refreshingly personal. *Talking with the Tarot* is a must-have for anyone looking to build a real relationship with the cards."

—**LISA PAPEZ**, author of *Unlocking the Tarot*

TALKING with the TAROT

About the Author

Samantha Rose Hicks is a professional tarot reader, witch, intuitive channel, teacher, and certified holistic coach. She helps individuals create a life they love through personalized tarot coaching sessions, available online and in person at her Atlanta, GA office. Samantha also hosts an online community where members can explore witchery, spirituality, and self-development—all in one place. Join the community or book a session at www.samantharosehicks.com.

TALKING with the TAROT

Conversations with Your 78 New Best Friends

Samantha Rose Hicks

WOODBURY, MINNESOTA

First Edition
First Printing, 2025

Book design by Rordan Brasington
Cover design by Kevin R. Brown
Interior illustrations by Llewellyn Art Department

Library of Congress Cataloging-in-Publication Data
Names: Hicks, Samantha Rose, author.
Title: Talking with the tarot : conversations with your 78 new best friends / Samantha Rose Hicks.
Description: First edition. | Woodbury, Minnesota : Llewellyn, [2025] | Includes bibliographical references.
Identifiers: LCCN 2024060451 (print) | LCCN 2024060452 (ebook) | ISBN 9780738778433 (paperback) | ISBN 9780738778495 (ebook)
Subjects: LCSH: Tarot.
Classification: LCC BF1879.T2 H53 2025 (print) | LCC BF1879.T2 (ebook) | DDC 133.3/2424—dc23/eng/20250205
LC record available at https://lccn.loc.gov/2024060451
LC ebook record available at https://lccn.loc.gov/2024060452

Llewellyn Publications
A Division of Llewellyn Worldwide Ltd.
2143 Wooddale Drive
Woodbury, MN 55125-2989
www.llewellyn.com

Printed in the United States of America

To my father, Ira, whose love of writing was just one
of the many gifts he bestowed upon me.
To my husband, Brian, whose love, patience, and unwavering support
allowed me the freedom to follow my dreams while placing his very own on hold.
To Ra, for always lighting my way, illuminating the joy and love
that is to be found in this life.

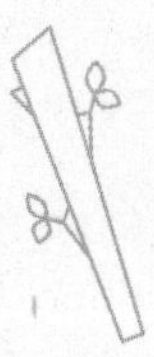

The High Priestess

Guardian of secrets, keeper of sight,
Illuminate these pages, mystic mother.
Through your veil, mysteries revealed,
Dispelling fears, a beacon's light.
Bless this work, your scrolls unfold,
In silence, wisdom flows.

Contents

Foreword

Elliot Adam

Tarot encompasses a dramatic cast of characters who reflect what is deepest and wisest within us. These timeless archetypes are humanity's oldest friends, bearing witness to our triumphs, tragedies, heartaches, and highest aspirations. We've known these ancient friends since humanity was painting them on prehistoric cave walls. Samantha Rose Hicks delivers a masterclass on how to connect with each ancient archetype on a deeply personal level. This lovely little book can help you interact with the cards, not as a pile of definitions to memorize, but as a gathering of old friends just waiting to get reacquainted. Samantha's unique method surpasses the act of absently reciting another person's card interpretations. Instead, she encourages you to listen—to truly listen—to what each tarot archetype is recalling in your own life experience.

Samantha's approach to tarot is warm, down to earth, and conversational. Her grounded voice is like that of a reassuring friend—personable, inviting, and full of wisdom... so appropriate for a Libra sun with Capricorn rising! She makes the mystical accessible, turning the act of pulling a card into a moment of personal discovery and connection. You are so lucky to have her accompany you through the hills and valleys of the Fool's journey as she provides kind introductions to the diverse archetypes you'll encounter along the way.

Many tarot study methods focus on condensing a card's meaning into several keywords that are rattled off when you see a corresponding card. Although this flashcard method effectively works for some, it can feel overwhelming for a beginner. It also glosses over the deeply personal dialogue that tarot symbols offer. Skimming the surface of tarot card meanings can have the unintended effect of detaching the seeker from authentically connecting with the cards. This book reveals that the tarot's story has always been your story. As you befriend each card, you are in fact recalling the highest highs and lowest lows of your own personal history.

Talking with the Tarot is rooted in the belief that everyone, regardless of their experience level, can find guidance, reflection, and insights through tarot symbolism. Samantha doesn't just teach you the meanings of the cards; she invites you to explore your own experiences and emotions through them. The cards are presented as a mirror, reflecting your innate personal wisdom back to you.

Whether you're new to tarot or have been consulting the cards for years, *Talking with the Tarot* offers something valuable. It's an invitation to slow down, to reflect, and to engage in a dialogue with yourself through the ancient, yet ever-relevant, language of symbolism. As you explore these pages, you will discover that you've known each archetype all along, and that you don't need "to learn" what each card means. You simply need to remember what the cards reflect within you. Get ready for an exciting, guided tour through the tarot's rich landscape as you journey back toward the wisdom found within your own history.

Blessings,
Elliot Adam
Author of *Fearless Tarot* and *Tarot in Love*

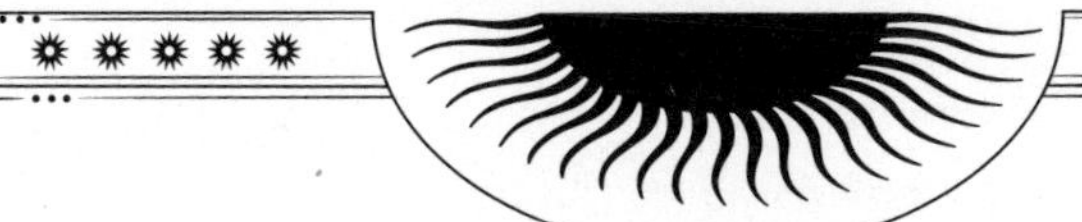

Preface

Dear beloved reader,

It is such an honor to meet you and be part of your tarot journey. Before you begin connecting with the tarot in a unique way, I wanted to first share with you how this book came to be and how one simple conversation sparked my entire tarot career. At the time of this writing, I do not have over twenty years of experience in reading the tarot, and that simple fact almost stopped me from feeling like I had a place in its world. As though I couldn't possibly have any knowledge to share with you because I hadn't earned that right through decades of dedication. But before I allowed this reality to stop me entirely, I grabbed my cards, performed a reading, and was reminded of a simple truth: the tarot doesn't care about the longevity of time spent performing readings, only I do.

When I performed my first tarot reading for a stranger, I had no idea what I was doing or what an incredible new life I was beginning. I had volunteered to help a friend sell her crystal jewelry at a local psychic fair, and I thought, Why not bring my cards with me? Maybe someone there could teach me a few tricks of the trade. I was sitting at my friend's booth in a corner by myself, attempting to shuffle the cards as a way of self-soothing while hundreds of people passed. I was unprepared for the large number of people and the loud noises emanating from them.

As I struggled to look like I belonged, this caring woman who smelled like lavender and rosemary came up to me and said, "Hey, can you pull a card for me?" I stared at her, completely paralyzed in fear. It was like time had stopped, and all I could do was look up at her, terrified, as I got bombarded with thoughts like, "What are you going to do? You're not a professional! Everyone is looking at you and will know you don't know what you're doing! She's going to make fun of you! You're going to make the real professionals mad!" I guess I wasn't very good at hiding my fear because even though it felt like time had stopped, it hadn't, and she laughed at my very shocked expression and said, "You don't have to. I just wanted to see if you were interested in pulling a card for me," she smiled, and my Southern politeness forced me to do the same. It also forced me to blurt out, "I'm not a professional. I am just here to help my friend, but I would be happy to pull one for you."

"Wonderful," she said sweetly. "Do I just pull one from the top?"

I attempted to reshuffle the cards; it was even worse with her looking at me, and I fanned out as many as my tiny hands would allow. This looked like I was a show magician asking her to pick a card, any card, but hey, I'd told her I wasn't a professional. She looked at the cards and pulled the Empress. My throat filled with sand as I struggled to tell her the card's meaning. A card I had gotten to know very well but, at that moment, felt like a complete stranger.

I looked up at her, swallowed my sand, and told her with fake confidence, "That's the Empress; she is the loving mother of the tarot and symbolizes fertility and the natural world, and is a reminder to nurture yourself because you're the soil in which the garden of your life grows." She looked at me and smiled but didn't say anything for, realistically, probably half a second, but it felt like ten minutes to me.

She touched her belly gently and said, "Hey, that adds up; my soil is growing a little seed right now."

Like a lightning bolt, shock and disbelief struck me. I couldn't believe it! I had never experienced this intense emotion before during a reading. Before the fair, I'd practiced as much as possible with family and friends, but it had never felt like that. And before I could even process what had just happened, she reached for another card, pulling the Three of Wands.

"Are you moving?" I asked her nervously.

"Yup!" she said happily with a smirk on her face. "Since you know we are growing our garden, we need more space."

"Oh, well, perfect, because this card *can* mean moving, but it can also ..." As I attempted to frantically give her the other meanings about the Three of Wands that I had memorized, she turned around, thanked me with a smile, and stated she had to go as it was her turn with a professional psychic. And just like that, I had performed my very first reading for a stranger and, in turn, stumbled into my destiny. That reading is the foundational point, the very roots, of my tarot career and, if I am being honest, the sprouting of my true life.

One moment, one conversation, and my life was forever changed. After that moment, something changed in me. Was the reading perfect? No. Would I go on to have hundreds of other readings that were also imperfect? Yes. But because of that moment, I had broken through the wall of fear and anxiety that surrounded me and kept me prisoner from truly moving forward in a life I knew I had always wanted. I wanted a life where I could do something I love and help people while doing it.

That reading took a hobby I enjoyed and transformed it into the career I was destined to have. The next day I emailed the founder of the psychic fair and asked her the requirements for becoming a reader. I told her I wasn't a professional, of course, but she took me under her wing anyway. That is where I was exposed to hundreds of different people, reading methods, and more. It was like I had jumped into the deep end of a pool, but it turned out to be the ocean. This exposure caused me to work through all my internal fears that came with being a reader and forced me to trust two things: myself and my connection with the cards.

Fast-forward to years of working at psychic fairs, private events, and now having my own reading space. I had this funny realization about my method of reading. Every time, no matter who I was reading for, I introduced them to the cards. I would let them know who the cards were, what they had been through, and how the cards' experiences would relate to the client's own. To me, this was completely normal, but a few of my reader friends let me know that this *is* a different method of reading the tarot. Other readers in my life would focus solely on the client in front of them. Relaying messages such as, "You're going to be getting a promotion at work," or, "Your significant other is hiding something from you."

I would provide the clients with similar messages, but it would always come with the addition of letting the clients get to know the cards. Some clients loved this as they felt it deepened the connection with the reading and provided more authenticity to the whole experience. Some didn't really want the backstory and just wanted the messages. Either way, I realized that the cards were more to me than just images on paper and that I had gotten to know them in an intimate way. My mind needed their stories, their histories, and it needed to share them with those around me, and now with you.

So that is where we will start. I will share the stories of the tarot with you, all seventy-eight. I will introduce you to every single persona as they introduce themselves to me. You will connect with them on a deeper level, and because of this, you will be able to see yourself within them. Allowing for real conversations and friendships to blossom leading to introspection, empowerment, and enlightenment.

A conversation once changed my life for the better. May I provide you with the same experience during this writing.

With all my heart,

Your tarot bestie (Samantha Rose Hicks)

Introduction

There is one thing that both a friendship and a tarot practice need to be successful: a solid foundation. Friendships build foundations through shared experiences, empathy, and trust. However, when it comes to tarot foundations, they are often based on a broad range of meanings and quick memorization methods. I want to change this approach for you, using the same principles that build lifelong friendships to create an unshakable connection with the tarot. I aim to do this by teaching you a conversational method of reading the tarot. I take the same elements that friendships thrive on—sharing experiences, empathizing with each other's perspectives, and showing up to build trust—and use them to facilitate an environment where the tarot becomes real to you: real people, real moments in your own life, real connections that can be felt no matter which deck is being used.

In this first chapter, I will share the intentions behind this book, explain the conversational method of reading the tarot, and explain how it will develop into a beautiful connection with the cards that will yield real-life results. I will also provide you with a summarized version of what the tarot is and how it came to be.

Why do I believe it is essential to share my intentions with you, explain to you how you're going to benefit, and take a quick walk down tarot's memory lane? Well, because I believe that intentions are the roots of our actions, and I want you to know what mine were when I was manifesting this book being held in your hands. I also think that it's important to talk about the benefits of stepping out of one's comfort zone to try something new, even if it seems intimidating. Lastly, I want to include at least some history of what the tarot is and its creation story because there is magic in the origins. Not everyone who reads this book will be a seasoned tarot reader. Some will be beginners, dabblers, and so on. Therefore, it would be a disservice to them to not include at least a brief overview of the tarot's history to provide context that will enrich everyone's understanding.

So, what are my intentions for this book? My intentions are to provide you with a fresh, immersive, and sustainable approach to reading the tarot. I want to create a world where tarot becomes your friend, a conversational partner, and you can feel safe, seen, and understood. Instead of feeling massive amounts of pressure to memorize meanings and force false feelings of affinity, these pages give you space to form real heartfelt connections. Whether you are a novice taking your first steps into the world of tarot, an intermediate practitioner looking to deepen your understanding, or a seasoned professional seeking a different approach, this book is designed to meet you where you are and guide you along your journey.

What Is the Conversational Method?

The conversational method is a three-step approach to reading the tarot.

The first step is introducing you to all seventy-eight cards as individual personas. Their personalities, their environments, who they are at their core. This will make them real to you and hopefully shift your mind from just viewing them as pieces of art.

The second step is providing you with the space to form connections with those personas by relating their experiences with your own. Imagining yourself in their shoes, sitting where they sit, seeing what they see—and then connecting those sensations with moments you've experienced in your own life.

The third and last step is performing a reading where you are speaking with the cards instead of at them. The reading should feel like you're having a conversation with friends instead of distant figures on paper.

How will this method help you? If you are like me and the many other readers I know, memorizing the cards' meanings and everything they are associated with can become a mountain that feels too steep to climb. You try, sure. You may even try repeatedly but never quite reach the top. This might make you feel like a failure or an impostor among experts, but I am here to tell you that you are none of these things.

It's not what you are doing that isn't working, but possibly the method you are going about doing it. We all think differently. Some are amazing at memorization and can retain or recall said information in a heartbeat for years to come. Me? I can memorize it for a moment or for a quick test, and then it's gone forever in the wind, never to be seen again. This felt awful when it came to reading tarot! I wanted to be a professional reader and empower people, but how could I do this effectively if I was struggling to recall what I had memorized?

This is when I found my way of getting to the top of the mountain. I had always treated the cards as if they were my friends. I learned all about their backstories, their experiences, and how, no matter the question, those experiences would show up time and time again.

Every time the Fool came into the reading, their childlike energy would be the same. The Fool would ask me to release, be brave, and take that leap of faith. It didn't matter if I was asking them about a job or even a way to better work with my shadow self. The core of who the Fool is was always the same, as was their story. It's their story that would keep coming back to me, not their ten different meanings depending on the context of the pull. The Fool became real to me, a real person I was going to repeatedly for advice; they had become my friend. I had learned the roots from which their advice would grow and then connected my own experiences to them.

Will every card pull provide you with the same advice? No. The advice will vary based on the context of your pull, but what will be the same is the root of the card's persona. This is where you will build your own foundations by connecting to theirs, relating them to your own, and strengthening your bonds to one another every time you perform a reading.

Another example is Justice. Justice will always provide you with advice from a rooted foundation of truth-seeking. No matter the context of the pull, their advice or "meaning" will always come from a place of absolute truth because it is who they are.

This is why the conversational approach is beneficial because it creates a core foundation for you without feeling like a chore or test. You first get to know the cards as real individuals you can relate to, and once that relation has set in, personal bonds are created. These bonds will allow for a stress-free reading experience because you won't feel the pressure that comes with having to recite information you have no connection with. Your intuition will begin to speak aloud, and the card's meanings will finally start to resonate within you. This is how real-world results will be created. If you take a chance and stay committed to the conversational method, you will soon feel empowered, confident, and, well, capable of endless possibilities.

The History and Evolution of the Cards

For you to connect with who the cards are now, I want you to take a moment to see who they used to be and how they evolved through time to become your new best friends. Would you believe me if I told you the tarot is as old as the Renaissance? Well, it's true, and it could be even older. Now, when I say the tarot, I do not mean the tarot that you and I use today, but its predecessor. The tarot we use today evolved from initially being a popular card game named *tarocchi* in Italy during the fifteenth century. This is the most accepted and widely told origin of the tarot, even though I have seen other resources connecting its beginnings to Egypt and even Asia, but that information is beyond the scope of this book, so I encourage you to do a fun dive into the time before *tarocchi*.

Wondering how the tarot went from a fun card game to one of the most beloved divination tools in the modern mystic world? For this evolution, we owe thanks to Antoine Court de Gébelin and Jean-Baptiste Alliette, also known as Etteilla. During the 1700s, both men embraced and publicized the mystical connection of the tarot, igniting a spiritual fire that still burns to this day. Court Gébelin is famous in the mystic community for linking the tarot to ancient Egyptian secrets and magic, but he was unable to provide any evidence of these connections. However, Etteilla and other mystics at the time didn't need proof of the tarot's relationship with the divine. Etteilla, who had already been using the cards for divination, further solidified tarot's mystical reputation by releasing his own tarot deck with hermetic associations, reinforcing the cards' esoteric significance.

This created a chain reaction in the esoteric communities, leading to one of the most well-documented occult societies, the Hermetic Order of the Golden Dawn, to get their hands on the cards and add even more fuel to the cards' spiritual fire. The order was so influential on the tarot that the very deck we will be using during this book was created by one of their members Arthur Waite and artist Pamela Colman Smith back in 1909.

Was this the very first tarot deck published for divine wisdom and spiritual transformation? No. Is it unrivaled in popularity? Yes. I personally credit the Rider-Waite-Smith's immense popularity to its artist, Pamela Colman Smith, because she captured something that no other deck during that time was able to do: the human experience. With her vivid colors and relatable scenes, her artwork revolutionized the tarot world. Pamela's art created its own revolution by sparking the other artists in her time and beyond to create countless deck variations that allowed for their own personal interpretations. I genuinely believe that is why the tarot is still alive to this day. The art spoke to us not only on a human level but on a soul one as well.

By the twentieth century, the tarot had undergone hundreds of transformations from a form of future-telling to now, a mirror into the subconscious. With the help of the internet, the tarot was able to reach previously unimaginable audience sizes, breaking down all geographical barriers. It was available to the entire world, and boy, did the world accept it. The internet allowed tarot communities to form not only in person but online as well. The tarot was unstoppable, and so were its interpretations.

The tarot has become a universal language, using its archetypes and symbols to speak to us. It holds up a mirror to our experiences of loss, love, growth, and spiritual transcendence. It doesn't care where you were born or what language you speak. The tarot steps forward as a tool for universal connection. We see our reflections within the cards every time we call upon them for clarity, perspective, and direction.

The tarot is now our sacred space, our tool for empowerment and authentic self-expression, but I want to take a moment and acknowledge that this did not happen without sacrifice. Throughout history, several marginalized communities have suffered unimaginable hardships, all in the name of practicing their spirituality freely. If not for their sacrifices, the tarot as we know it would not exist.

I want to acknowledge the Jewish and Romani communities in particular. The influence of Judaism on the tarot is clearly visible in the Rider-Waite-Smith deck, in addition to decks still being created to this day. The integration of Kabbalistic symbolism is a crucial part of the tarot's role as a tool of deeper understanding and spiritual exploration. But even though the Jewish community has been such a large contributor to the spiritual space, they still face discrimination and persecution. Thus, to honor their invaluable influence on mysticism, we must denounce hatred directed toward their community.

In addition to the solidarity we show the Jewish community, we must also stand with the Romani people. Generations of Romani have suffered continued discrimination and marginalization for us to practice divination openly. It is because of their way of life—their travels, their tribulations, their unyielding dedication to spirituality—that cartomancy is able to be so commonly practiced. It is because of these communities' hardships and so many others that we have the right to practice our own spirituality openly. They paved the way for us, so let's take a moment and thank them all humbly.

While I wrote this book to teach you a different way of connecting with the tarot, I am but one voice. I have used it to give you a very short summary of the tarot's complex history, but be adventurous; embark on a quest for deeper tarot knowledge to enrich your own spiritual practice. I encourage you to seek out diverse authors from marginalized communities. They will show you spirituality through their eyes, broadening your understanding of the cultures and religions that have shaped the tarot. Doing so will allow you to enhance your readings, infusing them with empathy, cultural sensitivity, and a deep appreciation for those who have struggled in the name of inclusivity.

Together, we can have the meaningful conversations that honor the past and create a diverse and compassionate tarot community for generations to come.

Chapter One
Understanding the Tarot's Structure

Now that you know the history of the tarot, I want to share its structure with you. Because you are trying to build a solid foundation with the cards, I want to make sure you know all the inner workings of the deck.

When I was first learning the tarot, everyone in my life had a different opinion on how I should start, but one thing they all agreed on was that I should start with the Rider-Waite-Smith deck. I won't lie: I wasn't attracted to the Rider-Waite-Smith deck at all. At the time, it just couldn't grab my attention, and it didn't help having everyone in my life saying, "Oh, you have to start with this deck; it's the best for beginners." That made me want to stay away from it even more, as if I was partaking in some rebellious act against my mentors. And to double down on this act, I decided to start my tarot journey with a random deck I found in a bookstore. It was beautiful, sure, but I had no real connection to it, even though it was my *first deck*. And because of my little rebellion, as I grew deeper into my tarot practice, I found myself desperately searching for *the deck*, the one that would speak to me and make all my readings finally make sense.

And then years later, on a random day, my husband heard a knock at the door and said sweetly, "It's here!" He opened the door, revealing a small box, then gently placed the package in my hands and said, "I didn't see this one on your shelf." By the time this surprise deck found its way into my life, I had collected over twenty different decks, treating them as if they were fine art pieces not to be touched. But as I unwrapped this loving gift, a feeling washed over me, and I knew. I knew this deck was *the one*.

Revealing itself to be the Rider-Waite-Smith deck, I found my little rebellion ending in a very anticlimactic way. The Rider-Waite-Smith deck may not be the prettiest or the one with the most elaborate backing, but it turned out to be the perfect deck for me. The one in which the figures on the cards were able to truly speak a language I had been struggling to understand. The colors of each card danced in the reflection of my eyes as the true essence of the cards began to come forward, penetrating deep within my soul. Believe me, I was bummed that my rebellion phase had ended so abruptly, but the universe does have its own plan, doesn't it?

With reluctance in my heart, I began to use the deck: first in my own readings, then with my family, and then with my friends. Shuffle after shuffle, it did not fail me. Bending to my small hands and terrible shuffling skills, it never disappointed me. This was infuriating as I wanted to be different and wanted to truly hate the deck, but it made it impossible to do so. Not only did the cards feel wonderful in my hands, but they were so much easier for my loved ones to connect with. The images, the colors, the symbolism, it was all so easy. After several months and many, many readings, they became my primary and have continued to be my primary for my clients even at the time of this writing. I now have a personal deck that I use when I perform readings for myself, but even that deck is based off the Rider-Waite-Smith.

I share all of this with you because I now have an unwavering connection to the Rider-Waite-Smith deck and will be using the card images from this deck as reference material for you in the upcoming chapters. I know, I know; you've probably read so many books that do the same, and I apologize if this feels redundant, but to stay authentic to my practice and my method of reading, it must be the Rider-Waite-Smith deck. The Rider-Waite-Smith deck will allow you to truly understand the tarot's personas and connect with their imagery and chosen language of symbolism.

Now, don't get me wrong—my collection of tarot decks has grown to over fifty decks and counting, but to this day, when performing readings for others, I reach for my Rider-Waite-Smith deck. The connection you are about to make is real, so if there is any resistance to this deck of choice, please don't let it stop you from moving forward. Remember, you do not have to use this deck in your own tarot practice, you do not have to be gifted a deck for the readings to resonate with you, and you do not have to start with the Rider-Waite-Smith deck.

The Rider-Waite-Smith deck is just the deck I will be using in this book to introduce you to the personas of the tarot. The connections you make with them have no barriers, so you will be able to transfer these connections to any deck of choice. Use the deck that calls to you and use the method you learn here to bridge any gaps.

Breaking Down the Deck

The reason I genuinely love the tarot is because it's a pictorial reflection of the human experience. I mean, how do you create something that was meant to be a mere card game, and it evolves into this incredible mirror of our entire existence? From our material needs to our emotional well-being all the way to our foundations of faith and the ever-looming fear of death. These are experiences we all share; no matter where we are from, these are the connections that bind us.

To express these experiences, the tarot was split into two separate sections: the Major Arcana and the Minor Arcana. You may hear them referred to as the trump cards and the pip cards, but for simplicity, I will be referring to them as the Major and Minor Arcanas. When meeting the Minor Arcana, you will connect with four different suits: the wands, the cups, the pentacles, and the swords. Now, before you close this book and say to yourself, "This is already too much," I want you to humor me. Remember, the cards reflect life, and because of this, I want you to see the four suits as four different areas of your life.

The wands reflect the areas of your life that you are passionate about, your creative projects, your sex life, and your spiritual self. The areas in your life that make you light up and bring you pleasure.

The cups reflect the areas of your life that connect with your emotional side. Your relationships, your dreams, your intuitive self. The deepest parts of you that flow inward and outward.

The pentacles reflect the areas of your life that root you in this earthly world. Your career life, your finances, your homelife, your physical self.

Then we have the swords. The suit that reflects your mind. It connects to your mindset and what lies within your thoughts, the way you speak to yourself and others, as well as your truth center.

Not so scary, right?

Now that hopefully I have helped you remove any fear of the Minor Arcana, I want to talk about the last four cards present in every suit: the court cards. Before my method of turning every card into a persona, the tarot already had sixteen personalities of its own. You could say its personal royal families.

Within each suit, there are four court cards: the page, knight, queen, and king. This means that you will be meeting a Page of Wands, Knight of Wands, Queen of Wands, and King of Wands, and this pattern is repeated for each suit. I know this may feel overwhelming at first since connecting with seventy-eight cards is already a mountainous task, and having sixteen court cards that all look very similar might make it feel even more daunting. It may seem impossible, but I am here to assure you that if you continue to read these pages, you will be able to connect with all these figures.

The court cards are the original personas of the Minor Arcana. They tend to represent people of influence in our lives and personalities with experiences of their own. They are rooted in the attributes of their suits: earthly matters, emotional maturity, passion projects, and quick decisions. This is exactly what we are learning when it comes to all the cards of the tarot with the conversational method, so meeting the court cards in this way as well is going to be a breeze.

Speaking of meetings, let's talk about the Major Arcana. This is the section of the tarot that screams *main character energy*. The Major Arcana is made up of twenty-two well-established archetypal figures who are unwavering in their being. Don't understand what *archetypal* means? I didn't either, so to simplify it, an archetype is a model or original of what they represent. If you feel a little confused on what that means, ask yourself what an emperor looks like. What qualities does he possess? If you were to take this image and place it on top of the Emperor in the Major Arcana, they would most likely match up. That's the point. The Major Arcana was created in such a way that no matter where you are from, if you think about an Empress or the Moon, the images and characteristics of the cards would match up. They are the blueprint!

I believe this is why so many find the Major Arcana much more accessible. They already have some subconscious connection with the archetypes, so it's a smoother transition to create bonds with the cards. Because of their archetypal status (main character energy), they have a larger or lasting impact on the conversation when performing readings, while the Minor Arcana brings transient insights through everyday experiences. In later chapters, we will perform spreads with a mix of both Major Arcana and Minor Arcana cards so you will see real-world examples of what I mean.

Understanding the Language of the Cards

Now that you are going to meet the cards as individuals, it's important that you understand how they will speak to you. The tarot speaks in the language of symbolism. Unsure of what symbolism is? That's perfectly fine! Symbolism, as I have come to understand it, is the use of something (an idea or object) to represent something else.

For example, instead of just saying the Fool represents purity, the Fool is holding a white rose in their hand. The white rose is a symbol of the Fool's purity. So even if you didn't know the meaning of the card because of its symbolism, you would be able to gather its meaning intuitively. Does that make sense? If not, let's do another example.

Let's say you were looking at the Ten of Cups card, and you see a rainbow. The rainbow to some may just be a beautiful colorful addition to the card, but to those who understand that the tarot speaks in symbolism, they would ask themselves what this rainbow could represent. Does it represent hope? Does it represent faith and trust in God? See, when it comes to the tarot, what you see on the cards themselves represents something deeper.

To help you uncover those deeper meanings, I encourage you to keep your Rider-Waite-Smith tarot deck by your side as a reading companion. As you meet each card, take a moment to bring the card forward and ask yourself these four questions:

- What are the colors of the backgrounds?
- What do you see going on in those backgrounds?
- What are the nonhuman elements shown?
- What are the humans doing on each card?

If you ask yourself these four questions every time you pull a card, you will become an expert in picking up the symbolism of the cards in no time. But I will also make sure to cover all these areas when introducing you. That way, it is more of a subconscious learning instead of a conscious stressful requirement.

Reading Reversal

Not only does the tarot speak in symbolism, but it also speaks in position pulled. When a card is pulled upside down, it is commonly referred to as a reversal. This also tends to feel like a roadblock for many new readers, so I want to put this disclaimer out there right now: *You do not have to read the cards as reversals.*

Hot take? It may seem that way, but it's not. Many readers in my life do not read reversals. This has always been a preference of choice for the individual reader. I personally know a professional reader who has been reading the tarot for over thirty years and hasn't read a card in reverse one day in her entire career, and guess what? No one has complained or canceled her in over thirty years. Reading reversals is a preference. This is why you will find the meanings of reversals to be so different from resource to resource. I view reversals in three ways:

The first way is resistance. This normally means that the advice being given from the cards will be resisted. Just like when your friend is giving you advice that you don't want to hear, even if deep down you know it's the truth.

The second way is blocks. Meaning that the card's persona can't be their truest self because something is blocking the way. Just like when a friend is having a bad day and acting the complete opposite of who they are. An example that comes to mind is when you have this bubbly, happy, enthusiastic person in your life, but you meet up and they are sad, angry, and just apathetic. Something in their life is blocking them from being themselves. When I get these types of reversals, I like to ask my cards what the block is and what actions I can take to remove it.

The third way is releases. I normally will only apply this viewpoint to certain cards, but again, that's because reading reversals is a personal preference. Some will not agree with this, but that is perfectly acceptable to me. Remember, this is your practice, and you will have to find what works best for you. When it comes to reading reversals as releases, I tend to apply this method to cards such as the Three of Swords, the Eight of Swords, the Devil, and so on. Cards that, when shown upside down, mean something is being released. Whether it be swords falling out or chains falling away.

I know all this can feel confusing, so you won't find any reversal meanings in this book. Instead, I've included reversal prompt questions based on the viewpoints shown above. My goal is for these prompt questions to ignite a conversation within you. Then later when engaging in readings, you will instantly recall your personal connections to the cards when shown in reverse.

All right; now is the moment you have been waiting for. Finally, meeting the cards as individuals. To begin this journey, you will start by hearing their stories and learning the ways in which their imagery speaks to you. I will be describing where they are coming from and how that origin will impact their advice to you. I will also be describing them as people in your life or real-life moments you may have experienced. I do this because it's easier to form a connection to the tarot when it is presented to you as someone you know, such as your stern traditional father, or a moment you have experienced, like the loss of a job.

I will then walk you through how they may appear in a conversational reading. This will be a general idea as the context of the card pull will always alter the advice, but not the roots from which the advice is given. I say this not to confuse you or discourage you but to allow you to open yourself up to all possibilities, which in turn will take the pressure off. This means you don't need to go in with the idea of perfect memorization because it would be impossible to do so.

Ahh, isn't it nice having that weight lifted? I hope so!

So, get somewhere quiet, allow your walls to come down, grab your deck of cards, and invite your intuition to come forward, because it's time to get to know your new best friends.

Chapter Two
Meeting the Major Arcana

From leaps of faith to breaking down old structures, the Major Arcana is filled with personas rooted in the milestones of life. As you meet these personas, think of them as guides connecting you to major events and energetic shifts happening throughout your lifetime. I invite you to take your time with each persona. Listen to their stories, place yourself in their shoes, and engage in conversation. Slow down, journal your connections, note any memorable feelings, and write down any insights that come forward, especially when reviewing the reversal prompts.

Choose to make each moment with the Major Arcana memorable by allowing their presence to resonate on a deep level. You have been where they are, you have felt how they feel, and now it's time to meet them and learn to recognize them in your real life.

0 The Fool

Have you ever met someone who is so innocently naive that you almost look up to them because of how stress-free they are?

Well, if you haven't, let me introduce you to the very first Major Arcana card, the Fool. You are meeting the Fool at the very beginning of their adult journey. They have decided to leave the safe and secure walls of their home and embark on an adventure of self-discovery and maturity.

They hold in their hands reminders of where they are coming from and where they are going. One is a white rose collected from home, reminding them of their innocence and purity when it comes to this world. They have not yet traveled or experienced any hardships, so the rose is in its purest form. In the other hand, they hold a satchel.

Is the satchel filled with goodies from home in an attempt to prepare them for the road ahead, or is it empty, in hopes that they will fill it with the experiences they collect along the way? The bright sun beams behind them with a golden yellow as if letting them know the universe is supporting them on their new adventure, illuminating the path to enlightenment. But the sun isn't the only thing the Fool can see; in the background, rows of mountains greet the sun, letting the Fool know this journey will be challenging but not to let the low points keep them from reaching the highest peaks of transformation.

As the Fool opens to their new life, you see their loyal furry friend reach out, barking, an instinctive warning that the Fool is getting close to the edge and, therefore, closer to their destiny.

Talking to the Fool in a Reading

When the Fool appears in a reading, they are going to give advice rooted from a place of adventure and playful release. Their advice stems from their foundation of freedom, universal faith, and blind trust. They are the persona of starting over without a plan, going with the flow, and having a fun time doing it.

You know, when you are speaking with the Fool, you are speaking with the playful energies of childhood. You are going to receive advice such as, "Just go for it!" and, "Hey, you don't need a plan; you just need faith it will all work out," or one of my favorites, "Trust your gut and do it scared!"

The Fool shows up in our lives when we need encouragement to start that new scary project or go out on a date with someone we just met. When we decided to create a resume because we are finally taking the leap and shifting our careers. Or when we decide to be spontaneous and go to the local dog shelter and pick up a forever furry best friend (true story).

Creating a Personal Connection

I want you to think of a time when you knew in your soul that it was time to start over but were scared to actually do it. Was it when you wanted to start a business but weren't sure if people would buy from you? Was it when you wanted to leave a relationship but were scared the other person would get upset? Was it when you wanted to write a book but were scared no one would like it? (Personal experience with the Fool.)

You will know you are connecting with the Fool when you finally decide in your mind that it is time to start something new and that decision brings up emotions of fear mixed with excitement.

Reversal Prompt Questions

Where is there resistance to release?

Is there a block when it comes to having childlike faith?

How can you release your need for control and planning of life?

1 The Magician

We all know someone in our lives who somehow gets everything they want. They speak their wants and desires into the world, and then *bam*! They get it! This is the Magician incarnated.

The Magician comes from a place of personal power and divine connection. You are meeting him in his workroom, where he is the most powerful because he stands in a place of his own creation. Around him are red roses and lilies, representing his connection to our earthly plane, but also representing the fruits of his labor. He planted the seeds, nurtured them, and through his passion and commitment, they now flourish.

He is a professional crafter. If you look at his worktable, you will see all the symbols of the Minor Arcana. The pentacle, the cup, the wand, and the sword. He uses all these as tools to create a life where he can thrive. His red robe draped over his shoulders, a symbol of power and passion. The infinity symbol above his head is deliberately shown in black so that you may see with your eyes his connection to Source. He knows he is connected, but he wants you to know this as well.

He holds a wand that mirrors his hands, reaffirming his ability to harness not only the energy of the divine but also the ability to use this energy to manifest his real-world reality. The Magician is the creator, and I want you to see him as a mirror.

Talking to the Magician in a Reading

When the Magician comes forward in conversation, his advice will be grounded in self-reliance. His advice will be rooted in his own experiences of using the tools you have to create the life you want. He understands his own power and what he can create from it, so when he comes forward, he will encourage you to recognize this power within yourself. He is the master of turning an idea into a real-world creation.

You will receive advice such as, "Use what you have right now and create something you love," or, "You have the power; what are you doing to do with it?" and even, "Allow yourself to be the conductor of both the divine and the earth. Center the energies within you."

The Magician is a man of active creation. He is a toolsmith with a master plan of higher purpose. When he enters the conversation, it's to remind you that you are part of Source, and Source is the creator of worlds. *You* are the creator of worlds.

Creating a Personal Connection

When was the last time you felt powerful? Not powerful in the way of putting others beneath you, but powerful in your own innate being? Like you woke up one day and said, "Yeah, I am *that*!" This is the confidence of the Magician.

Creating a personal connection with the Magician is to connect back to a time in your life when you felt so aligned with your purpose and you created something from that alignment. A time when you pulled together all your resources and remodeled your home to fit your truest self. Maybe a time when you stepped into your power and asked your boss for a raise, showing them all what you had accomplished. A moment when you looked at all your art supplies and felt that spark of creativity that gave birth to a masterpiece. Or when you stepped into your magic and performed a ritual that yielded real-world results.

These are all tangible examples of the Magician. Take a moment to connect with your own experiences where you felt like the powerful creator of your own world.

Reversal Prompt Questions

Where do you feel a block when it comes to self-confidence?

Do you have resistance when it comes to believing you manifest your reality?

What mindsets need to be released for you to own your personal power?

2 The High Priestess

In the stillness of her moonlit temple, secrets of the soul whisper to you through the High Priestess.

The High Priestess greets you as she sits in the in-between. She is an ancient being clearly, but as you gaze upon her, you feel a sense of familiarity. Her depth of knowledge is unimaginable, as is her power. Unlike the Magician whose power is fierce and loud, hers is passive and patient. She sits between two pillars, black and white, representing her duality and balance. She is both the darkness of the subconscious and the light of the conscious.

Behind her, a tapestry of pomegranates hangs, purposely displaying her fertility but also carefully covering the waters behind her. She does not need others to see the deepness of her or her magic. She does not need others to see her at all because she sees herself. The moon rests at her feet while the phases adorn her head. She wanes and waxes, seeing herself present in all the phases. The Torah peeks from her hands, representing all the hidden knowledge she contains as well as her roots in all things mystical and divine. She is the personification of the intuitive self and comes forward as the key to unlocking your own.

Talking to the High Priestess in Conversation

Talking to the High Priestess should feel as though you are talking to the deepest part of yourself. She appears when she knows it's time for you to connect with your own intuition—when you need someone to remind you that to disconnect from others is sometimes necessary to connect to your true self. Her advice is rooted in her inner wisdom. She will come forward with advice such as, "Turn off everything around you and tune in to yourself," or, "How do you feel about this? Don't look to others right now; tap into your own feelings about this situation," and, "You are magic incarnated; tap into this magic and strengthen your own intuitive abilities."

The High Priestess is the mystical intuitive psychic within us all. She is knowledgeable of things known and unknown. She is unwavering in her self-acceptance and reliance. She is the perfect persona to call upon when you need to be guided by intuition, not action. When you want to tune out the world and tune in to yourself, the High Priestess is your go-to companion.

Creating a Personal Connection

You can find the High Priestess in everyday moments, such as suddenly feeling like you should take the back roads only to find out there was a wreck on the highway. Moments when you are called to journal your inner thoughts or start a new spiritual practice that is just for you.

One of my favorite memories of connection with the High Priestess is when my husband and I were on our way home from the grocery store and suddenly my intuition told me we needed to visit the local animal shelter. We already had two cats, but something in me said a new furry friend needed us. So, I asked my husband to turn around, and with only a little confusion, he did. We ended up adopting the sweetest puppy named Goose who just so happened to be the only dog who got along with cats. I listened to my intuition that day even though it didn't unveil all the information I needed. I just knew. Our sweet Goose is now three and we couldn't imagine our family without him.

What experience is coming up for you when you think about a time you heard your inner voice? When did you just know you had to do something, even something as small as going to an animal shelter?

Reversal Prompt Questions

What is blocking you from connecting to your intuition?

Why do you have resistance to going within yourself?

How can you release the fear you have when it comes to looking at the magical side of yourself?

3 The Empress

Welcome to the garden of life. Here, sitting on her throne of abundance, is the mother of the natural world and tarot: the Empress.

The Empress greets you with a welcoming smile as you take in all she has created. The sun's warmth hits your face as you stand in the lush landscape of trees, flowers, and flowing water. The wheat around your feet represents the Empress's ability to grow all that is rich and plentiful.

The Empress is fertility and abundance manifested. She sits on a luxurious throne of red pillows and blankets, which ooze unapologetic passion and confidence. She wears a dress covered in red roses, symbolizing her fertile nature and beauty. She is all things beautiful. The crown of stars connects her to the universal energy of creation, while the scepter in her hand allows her to harness and direct that energy into the world around her. The heart-shaped shield is not in her lap to be used as protection, but beside her, facing you. She wants you to know how strong her feminine power is and how she has used this power to create all that surrounds you.

You are standing in her creation—the very soil in which her power gives birth to new life.

Talking to the Empress in a Reading

The Empress is always a mother first, so when she comes to speak with you, it will be from a mother's perspective. Her advice will stem from her maternal instincts and the love a mother has for their child. She will remind you that you are abundance and creativity incarnated. You must nurture yourself, others, and situations from a place of love. She will come forward with advice such as, "You can't grow a healthy seed in rotting soil; take care of yourself first," or, "Remember that all things need love and patience to grow, so whatever you are trying to create, make sure you are pouring love into it," and, "You are me, so all things from you can be born."

Creating a Personal Connection

No matter your gender, you can give birth and embody the energy of a mother. We give birth every day in our lives without even consciously thinking. Every time you create something, you are giving it life, from giving birth to a new human to starting an LLC. In both moments, you are embodying the energy of the Empress.

You can connect with the Empress in everyday moments, such as planting a small garden in your backyard or starting a new morning routine that focuses on self-care. You can even connect with her in moments like buying a new outfit that makes you feel sexy and unstoppable. These are all the different aspects of the Empress showing up in your everyday life.

I want you to think about a time when you embodied the Empress and how it made you feel. What were you doing?

Reversal Prompt Questions

Why are you resisting nurturing yourself?

What is the cause of this creative block within you?

How can you release the fears that are rooted in a scarcity mindset?

4 The Emperor

Do you remember meeting the Magician and him being the creator of his world? Well, let me introduce you to the ruler of that world: the Emperor.

A creator and a ruler can be very different in energy. As you can see when comparing the cards, the Magician and the Emperor are very different in colors, symbols, and overall appearance. The Emperor in his natural state is a very structured ruler. His main goal is to preserve what has been created so that it will last forever. He knows that a solid foundation will not crack. The Emperor is that solid foundation. Unwavering in his authority and logic, he is consistent with his dedication to his kingdom and the people who reside within it.

He sits on a throne of stone with ram heads carved into each corner, representing his determination as well as his connection to the fire sign of Aries. Though the Emperor is a man of fire, he is not the destructive fire we see burning down houses but instead the controlled burn of a forest so that new life can grow. He is fire directed and harnessed for future creation. There is a purpose and logic to his power.

He holds a globe in one hand and a scepter in the other, both as gold as his crown. He is the leader, the ruler, of the world itself. You see his cloak of powerful red but also the shiny glimmer of his protective steel armor. He protects himself and all that he has achieved. The background is filled with mountains, representing the challenges that he has and will continue to overcome.

You may be meeting him thinking, "Wow, this guy is serious and a little overbearing," but I want you to take a step back and look at his feet. There may not be any flowers, but there is a small stream of water. He does have feelings; he just chooses to not let them cloud his judgement. Do you feel like you are meeting your dad, grandfather, or boss right now? Good! Then you would be right. You are meeting the disciplinary of the tarot, and trust me, he does serve a purpose in your life.

Talking to the Emperor in a Reading

Why would the Emperor be a good person to talk to in a reading? This is a question I get asked often, and the honest reason is because we all need a little direction in our lives. When you talk to the Emperor, he comes forward to remind you of your own authority and asks how you can direct it. He is saying, "What could you build from this creativity if you only had some structure?" or, "You know you are the ruler of your life, right? Why are you letting someone else tell you what to do?" and, "If you put in the work now, the future gain will be measurable."

Creating a Personal Connection

When I hear the words *discipline* and *authority*, I instantly go, "Gross." But that may be my inner angsty teen coming out. As an adult, having these energies in my life has always yielded impactful results. Such as me buckling down to start my business and stepping into my power to set boundaries with people.

I want you to recall an experience where you stood up for yourself and did not waver in your beliefs. A time like when you had to stick to a routine knowing that would eventually yield rewards. Or when you had to give a public speech and force yourself to be confident and embody the authority figure of that subject. And maybe even a time when you had to remove yourself from a friend group because the relationships were not benefiting you but causing destruction in your life.

Did an experience come to your mind? Can you relate it to what you have learned about the Emperor?

Reversal Prompt Questions

How can you release the need for control?

What blocks are coming forward when you think about personal power?

Do you feel resistant toward authority?

5 The Hierophant

Are you seriously meeting another leader? Yes you are my friend, but this one doesn't lead society; they lead the soul.

Meet the Hierophant, the soul teacher of the tarot. We all have different people of influence in our lives, from our mothers, fathers, teachers, and possibly even spiritual mentors. The tarot reflects our human experiences, therefore it must provide a persona spiritual in nature. We are all spiritual beings to some degree. Some call it religion, others call it spirituality, and some may have an entirely different descriptor, but at the end of the day, most of us have a sense that we are part of something larger. That we are all connected to one another and to something unseen.

The Hierophant is here to guide you on that journey of connection and soul discovery. They are the bridge you take to connect to your divinity. They appear as an iconic priest, holding a scepter with crosslike imagery in one hand as the other hand points to the heavens. A crown of gold represents their authority about all things spiritual, while their red and white robe mixes the energies of leadership and purity. Below them, you see a pair of crossed golden keys as if they are the key to the universe itself, able to unlock it and lock it at will.

Below the Hierophant, you meet two figures who do not show their faces. They look up toward the Hierophant as if waiting for instructions. You then see the familiar pillars of balance and duality that caught your eye when meeting the High Priestess.

The manifestation of divine wisdom, the Hierophant steps forward as the spiritual mentor you seek.

Talking to the Hierophant in a Reading

Divinity has entered the chat. When the Hierophant comes forward to give advice, they do this from a rooted place of support and guidance. They are here to serve the needs of the soul. They are a teacher of all things spiritual, which means their advice may sound like, "Are you the one in charge of your soul's purpose or are you letting others lead you?" or, "You know others look up to you, right? Are you being the best version of yourself?" and possibly, "Do you have the right support system around you right now for your soul's development? Can you find like-minded people to talk to or even a mentor to seek guidance from?"

Commune with the Hierophant when you need a soul guide in your life. They will help you find your path to your inner divinity.

Creating a Personal Connection

You don't have to be spiritual or religious to have experiences that connect with the energy of the Hierophant. I think that can be a block for some people, so for those who can't connect to the divine aspects of the Hierophant, I want you to try to connect to the traditional side of them.

Think about a time when you had to conform to what others were doing. Maybe you bought clothes at a popular store not because you liked them but because everyone else was wearing them. Or a time when you had to bake a certain dish for a specific holiday because that was the tradition. Those are also real-life connections to the energy of the Hierophant.

Now, if you are spiritual, your experiences may be a little easier to recall, such as when you first went through your awakening and suddenly felt a calling to learn as much as you could about all things spiritual. Or when you found yourself leading a meditation group and everyone was sitting in stillness waiting for your next instruction. Maybe even when you realized for the first time that you had intuitive gifts and began to strengthen them and use them to help others.

What experience is coming to mind for you right now that makes you go, "Oh wow! That is definitely the Hierophant's energy!"

Reversal Prompt Questions

How can you remove the block when it comes to being independent?

Do you have some resistance toward seeking out a mentor or being seen as one?

How can you release yourself from the rules when it comes to spirituality?

6 The Lovers

A union of the heart takes a decision of the soul.

You are meeting the Lovers right as they are on the precipice of a life-changing decision. Do they form an impenetrable union, or do they maintain their individuality and walk away? As you can see, right now they are at arm's length from one another but are also somehow in unison. One is the divine feminine, standing in front of the tree of knowledge, representing our inner knowing of all things. The other is the divine masculine, standing before the inflamed tree of life, representing our connection to all things. To come together would mean to be in complete alignment with the universe, but the decision must be theirs alone, and based on the landscape behind them, they have quite a few obstacles standing in their way. Can they overcome these challenges together and meet in the middle?

It's important to acknowledge that they are not alone as above them in the beaming sunshine is the archangel Raphael, who is here to guide the two energies together and create harmony within their worlds. Archangel Raphael is the angel of healing and communication, so the two energies must do this before completing one another successfully. They must both make a conscious choice to heal their individual selves and then communicate with one another from a place of equality.

Talking to the Lovers in a Reading

Because you are meeting the Lovers at a time of choice, that is where their advice will stem from. Most of the time it will center around a relationship because that is who they are at their core. They are the two halves that make up a union. They will enter the conversation and ask you what options you have, and which one is for the highest good. You will receive advice such as, "Before you enter into this commitment, are you sure it is in alignment?" or, "You two seem to have very different views on this subject; is there a way to meet in the middle?" as well as, "Before you move forward, make sure everyone is getting what they need."

The Lovers are the go-to personas in a love reading because they can show you where things are in and out of balance, but they are not limited to these types of readings. The Lovers is the persona of all relationships, romantic or otherwise. I encourage you to seek their counsel when doing readings for self-love, business decisions, and more.

Creating a Personal Connection

You may have already formed a personal connection to the Lovers when meeting them by thinking about your own relationships, which is wonderful. But I want to expand on this example and allow you to go deeper.

When was a time you had to make a life-changing choice that would impact a relationship in your life? Did you have to commit to marriage? Or did you have to seek couples counseling to strengthen what was already there? Did you have the conversation about having kids and realize your partner was not on the same page, so there was a choice that needed to be made? Did a job opportunity come up that would require you to move, and you had to decide whether to stay in a relationship or move as a single individual?

Every day we make choices that impact others. Which ones are coming forward for you? When was the last time you had to weigh your options?

Reversal Prompt Questions

Is there a block within you that has trouble trusting another completely?

How are you resisting commitment?

What do you need to release when it comes to your relationships? Is it the other person?

7 The Chariot

You better move out of the way before you get run over, because the Chariot is passing through, and they are moving fast.

You are meeting the Chariot as they are embarking on their journey of moving away from all that is comfortable. As you can see in the background, they are leaving their home behind and are confident they will be successful. They aren't leaving spontaneously like the Fool and just wandering into the unknown; no, they have a mission, a plan. This plan is part of their soul's journey, illuminated by their divine connection, symbolized by the stars above them and a single star of hope placed on their crown. This journey is one guided by their inner voice, represented by the crescent moons adorning their shoulders.

They know what they are doing, and they are confident that this is the right decision. Protected in armor, they do not fear failure or loss as the scepter in their hands allows them to harness their strength and direct their energy forward. They have already been on the road to success, as you can see by them crossing over the water, which separates them from their home. They are on the move, and they won't stop until they have reached their destined destination. Carrying them are two sphinxes representing the Chariot's wisdom and ability to maintain balance when encountering obstacles along the way.

You have just met the embodiment of the saying, "Where there is a will, there is a way."

Talking to the Chariot in a Reading

Sometimes you must keep going, even if the only thing keeping you alive is sheer willpower. When the Chariot rides into a conversation, it's not to give advice of slowing down; it's the exact opposite. The Chariot is the persona of determined movement. When you seek guidance from them, you are tapping into your inner drive. They are going to give advice such as, "Remember why you are doing this? Don't focus on how you feel now; focus on how you will feel in the future. Keep going!" or, "Sometimes you have to do things scared, but don't let that fear stop you," and, "You can't get where you want to be if you don't make the first move; step on the gas and commit to your future success."

The Chariot is the ultimate hype persona for those of us who need a little extra energy in our corners, so find them when you need motivation to make a change or when you feel like giving up on a long-term dream. They will remind you of all the success you are capable of and your connection to your highest self.

Creating Personal Connections

Would you believe me if I told you the first time I was on a plane as an adult was when I was thirty-one years of age and I was going to another country? It's true! This was a big Chariot moment for me. I was terrified and had no idea what was waiting for me, but I boarded the plane anyway.

When was the last time you had to make quick and determined movements that may have been a little scary? Was it when you were moving out of your parents' house and into a college dorm? Or when you got your first apartment and suddenly had roommates for the first time? Did you shift careers even though the job you were leaving was safe and felt secure?

These are all moments shared with the Chariot. What moment is coming up for you right now? Sit here in this moment for just a little bit if you can.

Reversal Prompt Questions

What is a block you are currently facing that is slowing down your progress?

What resistance are you experiencing that is making you want to give up?

How can you release all distractions from your path and stay motivated?

8 Strength

Who is the woman petting a lion? Strength is her name, and she is doing much more than just petting it.

Known as the soother of all, even herself, Strength is the persona of fearlessness incarnated because she has mastered the ability to integrate with the divine. She does not fear anything because she is everything. Wow, yeah, I know that may be confusing, but stay with me. You see the infinity symbol above her head—it's just like the Magician's, right? She is connected to divinity and, therefore, to infinity. What happens to fear when you tell it you are connected to the infinite power that is the universe? It dissipates, losing all strength because it knows it has no power over you. You have tapped into your soul's strength and are now in harmony with your human instincts.

The lion in her hands represents those earthly instincts that all creatures of the world possess, such as fear, wildness, cruelty, and so on. But she does not run from the lion or even restrain it. She holds its head calmly and places her hands on it with grace and love, as shown by the flowers around her waist. The background is yellow with joy and confidence, as even the land around her is lush and fertile with greenery. Because she is tapped into the universe itself, her potential is limitless, as is her influence.

Talking with Strength in a Reading

Have you ever looked fear right in the eye and moved forward anyway? Well, then, you have met Strength. When Strength shows up to lend a loving hand, she is there to remind you how large you really are. She gives advice centered in her integration with source and her mastery over the primal being within us all. She will say things like, "Are you going to let the fear stop you or motivate you?" or, "How can you connect back to your soul center right now and take care of your own needs?" and, "What actions can you take to accept all the parts that make up you? Why are you suppressing them?" And possibly, "Do you know why you are triggered right now? How can you self-soothe in this moment?"

Strength is self-acceptance and self-restraint due to self-mastery. Wow, that's a lot of selves.

Creating Personal Connections

When I was creating a personal connection to Strength, two major events in my life came forward. One was the fear I felt when doing my first tarot reading for a stranger. If you read the preface, you already know how that turned out. The second occurred when a loved one triggered me, and I was on the verge of an air sign explosion. Instead, I grounded myself, attempting to self-regulate, and walked away. I could have started a fight to appease the justice warrior within me, but I chose not to. I walked away and recognized that the angry part of me needed something that only I could give her. I held back my animalistic rage that day and decided to tap into my true strength, which was mercy and compassion.

These are both examples of how Strength can show up in our lives. Can you think of a time when you had to show restraint or walk away and do some inner work? Was there a time when fear overwhelmed your body, but instead of freezing you moved forward toward your goals? Or have you had an experience that reminded you of how connected you are to the universe and, therefore, connected to a greater purpose?

Recall these experiences and affirm the energy of Strength in your life.

Reversal Prompt Questions

Do you have an inner block when it comes to feeling courageous?

How can you release the inner narrative that you are weak?

What resistance are you feeling right now when it comes to being self-disciplined?

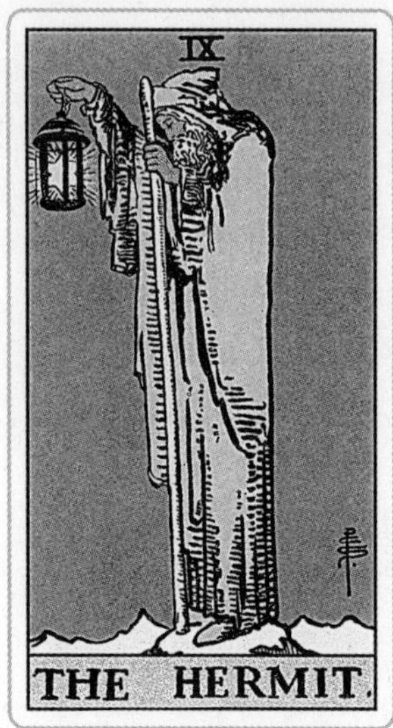

9 The Hermit

You will pick up on a theme throughout the tarot, and that theme is connection. Connection to self, connection to one another, and connection to Source or the universe. Here is when you meet the persona of self-connection through isolated introspection, the Hermit.

Looking at the Hermit, you can see there is not much around him. No buildings in the background or elevated landscapes, just him with snow at his feet. He is alone. Alone in the quiet dead of winter with only his staff, a lantern, and his cloak. His beard is long, signifying his wisdom with age as he leans on his staff for guidance and support. The lantern he holds up appears to be the only light source around as it beams with a single star of hope and inner illumination. He wears a long-hooded cloak as if hiding himself from the world around him. He does not look toward the empty space around but instead stares straight into the light. What does that tell you?

Talking to the Hermit in a Reading

When the Hermit comes forward in conversation, it is to advise you to take a step back. He asks you, "Is this environment around you constructive or destructive?" or, "When was the last time you checked in with yourself and didn't worry about other people?" and maybe even, "Can you take some time away for some self-care?"

The Hermit is not the friend to call upon when you want advice on how to build a better community, but he is the perfect person to ask how you can build a better you.

Creating Personal Connections

You know you are tapping into the Hermit's energy when you are tapping out of everything else. A personal connection that I will share about the Hermit is when I embarked on a stay-at-home silent retreat for a week. This was a conscious choice to remove myself from all noise for an entire week. No phone. No music. No people. Nothing. It was one of the hardest things I have ever done, but also one of the healthiest. It allowed me to reconnect with my own inner guidance system. To look at myself and the life I was living as if looking in a mirror and seeing it clearly for the first time. Were my habits healthy? Was I living a life in alignment with my soul's purpose? Was I even happy? These are the questions that one will find when embodying the Hermit's energy.

Think for a moment about a time in your life when you just had to step away. Did you take a break from a personal relationship? Or did you stay at a hotel for a couple of nights as a little self-care staycation? When can you recall a time when you just took a break from it all? And if you can't recall one, here is your invitation, my dear. Take a break.

Reversal Prompt Questions

What block is keeping you self-isolated? How can you return to the world?

Is there resistance when it comes to allowing others to see you? Are you afraid of rejection?

How can you release the mindset of being alone means being lonely? Where does that stem from?

10 The Wheel of Fortune

Ah, here you are, meeting your first nonhuman figure in the Major Arcana, the Wheel of Fortune.

This may suddenly begin to create a block for you visually, but I want you to take a moment and look at the Wheel of Fortune. Look directly in the middle of the wheel, right in the center. Do you suddenly feel as though you are staring into an eye? Good! That is how I want you to picture this card. You are staring into the eye of destiny right now—the personification of fate.

Look around the wheel or eye and see all the figures placed in the four corners of the card. Representing the fixed zodiac signs and portraying them with wings, alluding not only to the Wheel of Fortune's divinity, but also to its direct elevation from our earthly world. There is no landscape in the background, only the blue sky and white clouds of the heavens.

The Wheel of Fortune operates beyond our conscious control. At the top sits the blue sphinx, holding the sword that symbolizes our hidden thought patterns. At the bottom, we see the god Anubis, caretaker of souls who have shed their earthly forms, representing the cycles of creation. These cycles encompass the life and death patterns shared by all living beings.

Talking to the Wheel of Fortune in a Reading

When fate walks in the door, what do you say to it? When the Wheel of Fortune comes forward, it is to bring into question all things that appear consciously out of your control but are subconsciously under your command. It is to ask you what patterns you are repeating that are impacting your future and why you keep repeating them. It comes forward when you need to speak to someone who understands the larger plan and reminds you of the cycles of this life. The Wheel of Fortune can also step forward and reaffirm your connection to Source and the energy of luck that comes with that connection.

The Wheel of Fortune will offer advice such as, "Things are changing quickly around you; how can you stay centered in your purpose?" or, "What daily patterns are you repeating that are benefiting you and what patterns are harming you? Are you ready to let go of the harmful ones?" and possibly, "You are moving into a new season of your life—are you ready?"

The Wheel of Fortune is the perfect divine persona to bring forward when doing readings on major life changes that will require inner healing. If you want to talk to someone about a personal change that will impact your life moving forward, the Wheel of Fortune is a great confidant to call upon. If you are connecting to your spiritual side and doing spiritual development, the Wheel of Fortune will guide you back into the center of your highest self.

Creating Personal Connections

When it comes to creating personal connections with the Wheel of Fortune, I want you to think of two things: moments of little automatic behaviors and times when you felt things were divinely guided.

When I say moments of automatic behaviors, I mean moments like drinking coffee all day and forgetting to drink any water or staying up late until 2:00 a.m. and then sleeping in until noon. These are the moments when we take actions from our subconscious and aren't consciously present during them. The Wheel of Fortune doesn't necessarily ask you to change these patterns but to see them. To look at them as they repeat and ask yourself, "Are these taking me up or weighing me down?"

Can you think of a time when you suddenly realized a subconscious pattern was harming you and keeping you from moving forward with your goals? Once you have that connection, think of a time when things just worked out or you felt blessed and lucky. Where you thought to yourself, "Was that divine timing?" Experiences like running late for work but making all the green lights to arrive right on time for an important meeting. Or when you missed an opportunity but, in the end, you received an even better one.

Think about a time when things just worked out for you, and you were genuinely surprised.

Reversal Prompt Questions

Where in your life are you resisting change?

What block needs to be removed for you to ground yourself during the chaos?

How can you release your need for control?

11 Justice

You are meeting the judge and the jury as you enter the chambers of Justice.

Justice is the persona of complete truth. Most of the time, their truth is fair and brings balance into a very unbalanced world, but other times, people can view their truth as harsh or stern. The thing is, Justice does not care what others think or how others feel about them. All Justice cares about is being unwavering in their core values of honesty and integrity.

As you can see, Justice is a powerful being with a crown of gold to represent their leadership and a cloak of red reaffirming their power. They hold a sword, not toward the earth for protection, but to the heavens for discernment in all decisions. The scales of gold in their right hand show their connection to equality and the balance of life. Looking behind Justice, you see a tapestry of pure red, shielding Justice from a bright and sunny day. Justice does not face the sun as they need complete focus on the task at hand. They sit between two grey pillars of neutrality, just like the Hierophant. With no water present, we can see that Justice does not allow emotions to influence them, but only logic and reason.

Talking to Justice in a Reading

Things may be getting a little serious if Justice comes forward to have a chat. Justice is rooted in all things fair and truthful, which means their advice is going to stem from a place of integrity. This can come forward as, "Are you being truthful with yourself right now? Does this really sit in alignment with you?" or, "Hey, maybe you need to take some time to figure out what the fairest option is," and even, "Think about the facts not the feelings of the situation before you move forward."

Justice is obviously the go-to person when it comes to legal matters or any situation in which you want to discover the absolute truth. I personally love talking with Justice when I need help navigating my own inner truth about situations in my life.

Creating Personal Connections

Do you remember a time when you were brutally honest with someone? Yeah, you were embodying Justice in that moment, even if it was their harsher side. Justice shows up in everyday moments where we are honest and fair with ourselves and those around us. For example, moments when you speak from your heart and are unapologetic about how you really feel. Or when you have to stand up for another who isn't able to stand up for themselves. Even little moments like balancing your work life with your social life. All these real-life experiences are aspects of Justice.

What are some moments that come to your mind when you think about fairness, balance, honesty, and integrity?

Reversal Prompt Questions

What block do you currently have that is making you go against your core values?

Why are you resisting seeing the truth of the situation?

How can you release any biases you may have?

12 The Hanged Man

Suspended in peaceful surrender, a new perspective can be found when meeting the Hanged Man.

You are meeting the Hanged Man while in an act of self-sacrifice. He hangs there completely surrendering to the universe. His golden hair falls to the earth as a light of divine enlightenment shines behind him. He's wearing a blue shirt to represent how at peace he is. We see from his red pants that his pose gives him a sense of empowerment. He is here by choice. No one made him do this. In fact, you can see he has tied only one foot by design and strategically places the free foot behind him. He needs to hang in this position to see his situation from a different angle. The background is grey, showing you that he is in a neutral state of pause. The only greenery shown hangs above him, representing the potential growth that he will receive by performing this act of complete release and change in perspective.

Talking to the Hanged Man in a Reading

The man of looking at things differently is coming forward and asking you to see things from his perspective. When the Hanged Man comes forward, he does so with advice rooted in his point of view, a different point of view. He asks you to take a step back and see all the angles of the situation. He is the king of unattachment, so he's going to ask you to do the same. With advice such as, "Can you take a step back and remove yourself from this for a moment so you can gain clarity?" or, "What is the bigger picture here? What are you working toward?" and, "How will releasing control in this situation benefit you and/or transform you?"

The Hanged Man is the perfect guy to bring forward when control over a situation is not working. When you need to just let go and see what happens. When you need someone to remind you to look at the situation from another's perspective or need a reminder to take a breath and sit in the uncomfortable for a while, so that self-transformation may occur.

Creating Personal Connections

Can you recall a time when you just needed a time-out? When things were chaotic and you just couldn't handle it anymore, so you pressed pause on everything to gain a moment of peace. Yeah, things probably were still uncomfortable, and you wanted to bring order to the situation, but you just needed a moment to reset.

Moments such as pausing to empathize with your partner during a disagreement. Or considering all the angles of purchasing a home before making the commitment to switch from renter to buyer. Maybe even when you went through a transition from religious to spiritual and your whole worldview turned upside down. The Hanged Man shows up in everyday moments of pause, reflection, and shift in perspective.

Close your eyes and think about a time when you were called to surrender either yourself, a situation, or a point of view.

Reversal Prompt Questions

How can you release the fear of sacrifice?

What is blocking you from seeing from another's point of view?

Why are you resistant to awakening?

13 Death

Riding through the veil of transformation, Death brings endings that give way to new beginnings.

Have you ever met someone and thought, "Wow, this person just changed everything." If the answer is yes, then you have met the energy of Death. Death is the persona of endings that provide space for new beginnings. They were present on this journey before you even met them as the Fool. Death was right there when the Fool stepped off the ledge into their destiny. Wearing the same red feather, Death brings forward a message of metamorphosis. Death is not a persona of cruelty or rage but of mercy and beauty, as shown from the white rose on the flag they hold. Death does not sit on a throne but rides a white horse of purity, signifying Death's forever movement through our lives. There is no stopping Death from coming; endings are inevitable.

Look around in the background behind Death. What do you see? Do you see darkness and gloom? No. You see the sun rising brightly as if lovingly whispering to you that a new life is about to be born. Water flows in the background as a small boat floats along the surface. You are witnessing a transitional moment. A moment between two states of being. As you look below Death, you may see what feels like a gruesome sight, but I encourage you to look closer. There is no gore to be found here. Just symbols of the inevitable. All creations of the universe must die. No matter who or what they are, Death will greet them. This can be shown by the king who has lost his crown, the maiden who looks away, the priest who begs for more time, and the child who shows no fear but instead innocent ignorance as they look up at Death.

Talking to Death in a Reading

When Death rides in, you know they are here to speak to you about transformation. Transformation cannot happen without an ending. This can feel like a heavy person to talk to, but wouldn't you want to speak to someone who always wanted the absolute best for you, even if that absolute best comes at a painful cost? Death will come forward with advice such as, "It's time to let go of this situation and begin the healing process." or, "Are you ready to step into your highest potential? Then it's time to shed this weight of what is no longer serving you," and, "You need to move forward even if that comes at a loss. Nothing here is benefiting you."

Death may feel scary and may get a bad rep, but they are the perfect person to talk to when you know you are ready for a change but need a little encouragement. When you need someone in your corner who knows the grass is in fact greener on the other side.

Creating Personal Connections

You may already be flooded with personal experiences of endings that led to new beginnings, but just in case, let's talk about some that give off Death energy. One of the more recent times I sat with Death and talked was when I was pulling cards on a major career shift. I was comfortable in my previous position. The pay was good, the people were great, and the boss and I had a good relationship. So why was I pulling cards on career, then? Because I felt a shift in my energy. It was like I knew even though nothing was wrong, a change was coming. After speaking with Death and performing a spread, I knew it was time to move forward on a very scary new adventure. Change was coming whether I wanted it or not. I was scared, sure, but I knew this change would lead to a complete rebirth of my soul.

Death is not always a welcomed experience in our lives; it may even be a dreaded one, but it is an inevitable one. Think about a time when you had to quit your job even though you were shaking as you called your boss. Or a time when you ended a romantic relationship knowing it would devastate the other person. A time when you sat your parents down and told them you were moving out.

All these experiences encompass Death. When was the last time you felt this energy in your life? Where did it lead you?

Reversal Prompt Questions

Why are you resisting change?

What is blocking you from welcoming in self-transformation?

How can you release the past and embrace the future?

14 Temperance

As they blend opposites harmoniously, you stumble into the realm of balance, harmony, and inner alchemy—meeting Temperance.

You are meeting Temperance as they stand in their beautiful and serene sacred space here on earth. They are not flying high in the heavens but here in the physical world, guiding us toward a life of healing, peace, and magic. Looking at them, you can see their large red wings of power representing their divinity and strength. They wear a white gown of purity adorned with a red triangle in the middle of a white square. You can't help but wonder why the triangle is enclosed. Does the triangle represent fire and the white square is keeping the fire in balance, or does the white square represent earth and all that is grounding and stable? These are questions I want you to ask yourself and see what answers come forward.

In the hands of Temperance, you see two golden flowing chalices. Temperance is pouring water from one into the other, somehow in perfect harmony without either overflowing or running dry. As you look around, you see beautiful yellow irises representing the Greek goddess Iris, the messenger of gods, as an illuminating sun rises behind a winding path. This path greets you and welcomes you toward it, knowing the joy and happiness that awaits you, but before you go, notice that Temperance has carefully placed one foot in the water and one foot on land. They are in a constant state of balance and moderation. If both feet were in the water, they would be overflowing with emotions and unable to maintain stability. If both feet were on land, they would be too grounded and unable to go with the flow of life. They need to be right in the middle, always connected to both energies.

They need to be in equilibrium.

Talking to Temperance in a Reading

When Temperance steps forward, you are speaking with a divine messenger, and because of this, they will come from a rooted place of inner peace. Temperance is a wonderful companion to call upon when things are just too much. You are doing too much, the world is taking too much. Nothing is grounded or even. Temperance comes forward with advice such as, "Are you going to an extreme here? Why?" or, "How can you meet them in the middle on this? Is there a compromise that will make everyone happy?" and, "Have you taken a second to give to yourself as much as you are giving to others? What do you need to recenter?"

Temperance is the perfect persona to bring forward when you need to speak to an energy larger than yourself or the situation. When you need a piece of the divine to sit down with you and remind you to make decisions from a place of balance and inner harmony. You cannot pour from an empty cup, so please do not force yourself to.

Creating Personal Connections

Have you ever been in a situation where you know things are out of whack? For example, when you are studying day and night for a test but are neglecting self-care. This is where Temperance would appear and ask that you pour into yourself as much as you are pouring into your studies.

Temperance can also be found in those moments where you could just explode but aren't sure why. In the moments when you find yourself being overstimulated and must find your center. I find I step into the energy of Temperance every time I meet in the middle when it comes to my group projects. Sure, in my own perfect Capricorn rising world, everything would be the way I want it, but that's not how the world works. To allow others in your life is to allow them to express themselves, so compromises will inevitably need to be made and that's okay.

What experience is coming forward when you align yourself with Temperance? When did you have to balance out a situation or feeling? What experience in your life forced you to do something in moderation?

Reversal Prompt Questions

Why are you resisting moderation?

What block do you currently have that is creating an imbalance in your life?

How can you release the need for conflict? Where can you find peace?

15 The Devil

In the shadows of desire, you find yourself chained to your self-sabotaging thoughts by the Devil.

The Devil is such a well-known persona of the Major Arcana I find most people just skip over them because they already have such concrete knowledge of what they represent, but if you find yourself doing this, I want to encourage you to stay with me, and actually meet the Devil.

You are meeting them in their place of power, the shadows. The darkness makes it feel as though you have entered a void outside of time, but that is because you have. You are looking at the darkness within yourself, within all of us. With large grey wings and horns, you see not only how animalistic the Devil is but also the magnitude of his reach. His hands mimic the stance of the Magician as he holds one toward the heavens and the other toward the earth, but they feel wrong and perverted. As you look down, you can see what looks like a twisted representation of the Lovers. With horns poking through their heads, tails with imagery of their origin trees, and chains hanging loosely from their necks. They aren't forced to be here, obviously; the chains are loose, so why are they here? What is keeping them here?

Talking to the Devil in a Reading

When the Devil walks in, it's time for the self-denial to walk out. The Devil comes forward to speak about all things toxic. All they know is toxicity, manipulation, addiction, and the attachment to all three. The Devil is rooted in the darkest parts of us all. The parts of us that we hide and are ashamed of. They see these parts, and these are the parts from which they speak. The Devil gives advice such as, "The shame you are carrying is keeping you here," or, "The addictions you are struggling with right now will eventually take you into total darkness," and, "Are you in love or are you in lust? Who is manipulating whom here?"

The Devil may be a feared energy, but they are one that allows you to look at the darkest parts of yourself and learn to heal them. The Devil is the mirror to our deepest wounds that we must address before they infect our entire being. Bring the Devil card forward when you need someone to be brutally honest about your behaviors and what you are currently indulging in.

Creating Personal Connections

As you were meeting the Devil, your eyes may have widened as you thought to yourself, "Yeah, I have experienced that." If that's the case, that is amazing! Keep that up! If not, I want you to think about the activities you do in the dark. What are you ashamed of? What are you addicted to or find yourself overindulging in? Can you recall a time when you were maybe a little manipulative or controlling? Think about those inner wounds you don't share with anyone else.

Think about something you do that you know is bad for you. Or something that makes you feel powerless and weak, but you keep coming back. For me, the Devil showed up in my life as substance abuse. I am four years sober now, but it took me sitting in the Devil's dungeon for ten years to finally wake up and free myself.

What is coming up for you? What are your darkest parts, and how are they keeping you captive?

Reversal Prompt Questions

What actions can you take to release yourself from these toxic patterns?

What block needs to be removed for you to be independent?

Why are you resisting taking back your own power?

16 The Tower

Out of all seventy-eight cards, I feel none is more dreaded or misunderstood than the Tower.

The Tower is another card in the Major Arcana that is more of an energy than a person. Still, we will be personifying this energy to stay true to the conversational method. Think of them as the loud, unexpected guest who shows up to a party they weren't invited to, disrupts everything, but in the end makes the party even better.

You are standing in front of the Tower right when they are in the throes of a crumbling. The energy around them feels chaotic as lightning strikes the crown from their very head, and fire surrounds them. The sky is black with grey clouds, letting you know the fire of purification is still burning, as smoke fills the air. The lightning is bright yellow, striking the Tower with a sudden spark of awakened enlightenment. The crown of authority and power begins to fall to the ground, signifying the release of all control. The figures who were once so high and mighty fall to their inevitable deaths, filling them with a sense of helplessness. It is a bleak scene, but one that makes way for a resurrection.

Talking to the Tower in a Reading

The Tower is a violent persona; there is no denying that. They come from a place of destruction and bring destruction wherever they go. The thing that people tend to misunderstand about them is that they are not a malicious being. They get no enjoyment from uprooting the lives of those around them. They do this to force those around them into their purest and most aligned selves. When you hide behind the walls of false realities that sit upon a foundation built from self-sabotaging cracks, it is bound to crumble eventually. The Tower just happens to be the persona who brings in the storm. When the Tower pops in for a chat, they aren't really coming in quietly. They come with advice of getting prepared for the inevitable. Everything that is not serving you is about to fall away, so get ready. If you were sitting face-to-face with them, they would say things like, "Hey, I know you think that this is good for you, but it isn't, so let's remove it right now. No time to wait," or, "The mindset you have is keeping you in this dark place; it's time to reframe and let the light in," and, "I know you've worked really hard building up those walls to hide yourself from the world, but it's time to let people see who you really are, so I am going to loudly make all those walls come down."

The Tower may be the last persona you want to see or speak with, but no one can open your eyes faster to a situation that needs to be removed than them. Chat with the Tower when you are really struggling to let go of your harmful patterns. Lean on them when you feel you just need someone to show you the light at the end of the tunnel. Allow them to enter your life and destroy what is subconsciously destroying you.

Creating Personal Connections

Are you finding yourself a little hesitant to connect personally with the Tower? Hey, I get it; destruction is terrifying, but honestly, it happens every single day. The Tower shows up in the mundane moments of our lives. The moments when we sit and think, "Welp, that just ruined everything I worked so hard for." Moments like having an explosive argument with a friend or loved one that ends in a breakup. The breakup is painful, and all those memories feel like they are falling away, but it does give both people a renewed sense of freedom.

My first experience with the Tower was when my father passed away. You may be thinking, wouldn't that be Death? Yes, Death was there, but the Tower was the main energy in charge of that event. It was shocking, sudden, and life-changing.

We didn't think we would ever recover, but not only did we recover, the loss created a stronger bond between my family and me.

Now, I am not saying the Tower will always bring a family death; in fact, that is going to be a very rare association, but the suddenness, the shock value, that is what will occur more often than not. Such as your childhood friend moving away with only a week's notice or failing an exam that brought your entire grade down to a D even though you studied. A modern-day example could be you losing a ton of social media followers overnight and not understanding why. These all share the same energies: shock, loss of control, destruction, and hopelessness.

What experience is coming to your mind when you think of these?

Reversal Prompt Questions

Why are you resisting the undoing?

How can you release any fears that come with a fresh start?

What is blocking you from accepting the truth that things are crumbling?

17 The Star

Hello, Hope, or should I call you by your true name? The Star.

You are meeting one of the most beloved personas of the tarot, the Star. She is radiant, isn't she? Beautiful and free as she shows herself so openly and authentically. The Star has nothing to hide, as you can see from her lack of clothing.

She kneels under a bright star illuminating the lush world around her; it is her guiding light. You see her pouring water onto the land, nourishing it and herself. Watering both with life and what feels like renewed purpose. The Star is not greedy, though, and she does not just simply take from the pool of life but gives back to it. She waters what waters her, as she knows they are connected. You can see this connection by looking at her feet. Reminiscent of Temperance, she has one foot in the pool of life and the other grounded in the earth.

Talking to the Star in a Reading

When the Star shows up, you know it's okay to take a breath. She comes from a rooted place of renewal, hope, inspiration, and loving guidance. She will not bring chaos or violence but instead the opposite. She brings forth words of harmony and peace. When the Star gives you advice, it will sound like, "Wow, you have been through a lot; want to rest for a moment while you realign with yourself?" or, "You know if you give up now, you won't be able to receive all the blessings coming toward you," and, "It may hurt now, but it won't hurt forever; let all those heavy emotions out so the lighter ones can take their place."

The Star is the persona you want to chat with when you need a reminder that self-care isn't selfish. She is the friend who inspires you to keep going after the chaos because she knows there is something great waiting for you on the other side. Call on her when you need to see the areas of your life that are worth nourishing because they are nourishing you.

Creating Personal Connections

If you are having trouble relating a personal experience to the Star, I want you to think of a time when you felt refreshed.

Was it after you quit that job that brought you to tears every day, and finally, for the first time in a long time, you didn't cry? Or when you reaffirmed your faith in yourself by coming back into alignment with your true self? Was it when you finally gave yourself a spa day and allowed yourself to relax completely?

I experience the Star's energy every time I take a spiritual bath under the new moon. There is just something magical about it that brings forth the energies of cleansing, openness, renewed inspiration, and personal peace.

What experiences are you thinking of as you read that?

Reversal Prompt Questions

What action can you take to remove this block creating your lack of hope?

How can you stop resisting the idea that things will get better? How can you regain your hope?

What do you need to release to respark your inner inspiration?

18 The Moon

Walking in the dark realm of dreams and mysteries, you see all your subconscious truths illuminated by the Moon.

The Moon is the personification of all things mysterious, dark, and wild. She is the untamed feminine energy within us all. The one who invites you to check in with your hidden intuitive self. She is the deepest part of your subconscious, playing out its wildest fantasies inside of your dreams. You meet her here, in her play area, where she is free to do as she wishes. Shining brightly, she drives even the most tamed animals to madness. The waters beneath her move at her command as a deep-sea creature comes to greet her, reminding her just how deep her influence reaches. Lush greenery is below her, speaking to her connection with life itself as a yellow path illuminates for the initiates who hear her call to go farther into themselves than ever before.

Can you feel the wild within?

Talking to the Moon in a Reading

When the Moon decides to grace the conversation, you know there is something deeper going on below the surface. The Moon is notorious for being the card associated with inner work or shadow work. They can come up as a call to begin this work by going within yourself, even the parts of you that you have hidden. The Moon is also the opposite of Strength in the way that Strength asks you to tame your wildness within; the Moon invites you to let it out. The Moon will give advice such as, "When is the last time you let your hair down and went a little wild?" or, "I know you have been resisting this, but I think it's time to do some inner shadow work around why you feel the way you do," and, "To connect with your intuitive self is to connect with the world around you; go outside and connect with the energies of the earth."

The Moon is the witches' called-upon companion because it allows them to connect to the divine power of earth and spirit all at once. To tap into the ancient power that comes from freedom and release of self. Call upon the Moon when you wish to go deeper into yourself or when you want all that is hidden to be revealed.

Creating Personal Connections

Creating a personal connection with the Moon may be difficult for some because they may feel that these moments of wildness, inner work, and intuitive connection don't happen in the everyday, but I am here to show you that they do!

You connect with the Moon's energy every time you are dancing to your favorite playlist or just having a party all on your own. When you are singing at the top of your lungs in the shower and don't care what you sound or look like. The moments when you release yourself completely.

The Moon appears in our lives when we are journaling and diving deep into ourselves. Taking control over our own healing and looking at our inner reflection. The moments when we connect to our unconscious mind via breath work, meditation, and so on. The Moon is there in the moments when you know something just isn't right. When your intuition is telling you something but someone else may be telling you something else.

One of my personal experiences with the Moon is when I was with my previous partner before my wonderful husband. I was in the kitchen and just knew something was off. My intuition was alerting me left and right. So, I asked my partner if there was anything they needed to tell me. They said no, but beneath the surface, I could see something was wrong. Later that day, I was speaking to my girlfriend about the situation, and she shared with me that she had seen my partner's name come up on her coworker's computer and that they were messaging back and forth romantically.

In that moment, it was like all the energies of the Moon were flying in my face. The facing of fears, the clarity that comes from seeing through illusions, and the confirmation of my connection to my intuition.

Will the Moon always mean infidelity? No. Absolutely not. But when it comes to modern-day moments, I want you to think about when you released all restrictions on yourself and let loose. When you took time to do the inner work and when you heard the call of your intuition loud and clear.

Reversal Prompt Questions

What block is keeping you from releasing your internal fears?

How can you release your anxiety when it comes to the world around you?

Why are you resistant to inner work? Why does shadow work scare you?

19 The Sun

All things joyous and bright become clear in the shining rays of the Sun.

You have met so many different personalities on this journey. Some come from pain, others from love. Some bring advice of movement, and others recommend standing your ground. But now, you meet the persona of pure happiness, enlightenment, and wonder. You are meeting the Sun.

The Sun is clearly the happiest card of the Major Arcana. As you look at this card, you should allow yourself to soak in the radiant joy that can be felt, from the openness of the child to the vibrant yellow of the sunflowers behind them. Does this child look familiar to you? With their red feather, long red flag, and white animal companion? Is this not the persona that speaks to the transfiguration of the Fool and Death? I like to think so.

You stand before the Sun as they are riding forward in all their illuminating bliss. Arms wide open to the world with no fear or doubt in their mind. They are alive with childlike innocence and are bursting with positive energy. The horse they ride is white, representing how pure the moment really is, while the flowers in their hair show just how full of life they are. The Sun beams as if it is shining just for them, expanding this blissful energy to all those around.

Talking to the Sun in a Reading

To speak to the Sun in conversation is to speak to someone who will always show you the brighter side of the situation. The Sun comes forward when you need to be reminded of all the good things in life, shining a light on the blessings you currently hold while reminding you that more is on the way. The Sun's advice will always be rooted in the silliness of life and will ask you when was the last time you saw all the wonderful things this world has to offer. Where the Hanged Man sees things from a different perspective through self-sacrifice, the Sun sees them through self-illumination.

The Sun will bring forward advice such as, "How can we look at this situation from a more positive perspective?" or, "Let's open ourselves up to all the wonderful possibilities!" and, "You are surrounded by so many blessings. How can we ground in gratitude for them?"

The Sun is your go-to persona when you need to see the lighter side of situations. When you need to be reminded of everything positive and joyful. The Sun is also a great persona to speak with when you need clarity on where to direct your energy when it comes to gaining future happiness.

Creating Personal Connections

When you want to form a personal connection with the Sun, I want you to think of a time that lit you up from the inside out—a moment when you were so carefree and playful that it radiated to a soul level. Moments like singing your favorite song in the car with all the windows down and letting the wind flow through your hair. Or maybe when you and your friends went mini golfing and were having too much fun to keep score.

Suppose you are spiritual like me, then the Sun can be connected to when you went through your first spiritual awakening. That incredible moment of soul illumination and clarity where you could feel energy for the first time and see it all around you. My favorite personal experience with the Sun was when I did a kundalini awakening breath work meditation that sparked my own spiritual awakening. I could feel the energy within myself building and then expanding into the world around me. I had never felt so energized in my life! It truly changed my life and allowed me to expand my horizons when it came to my spiritual practice. It was a moment I will never forget.

What is a moment of experiencing the Sun that you will never forget? What is a moment when you felt so happy and free that you had to bookmark it in your brain?

Reversal Prompt Questions

What is a block you need to overcome to see the happiness around you?

How can you release your negative mindset?

Why are you resisting a mindset change?

20 Judgement

Can you hear the angelic trumpet? It sounds like your soul's purpose is calling, and Judgement is here to make sure you answer the call.

Meeting Judgement can feel overwhelming because, let's be honest, their presence is humbling. Looking at them, you see this giant divine being with wings of red representing their sheer mighty strength as they blow a horn so loudly it awakens the dead. With arms wide open and naked with nothing to hide, the people rise up to this call of purpose and embrace the message of ascension. Will you answer the call?

Talking to Judgement in a Reading

When Judgement blows into the conversation, it's time to stop playing pretend and wake up to what you really want. Judgement is that friend who reminds you of your greater purpose on this earth and to break through all the noise. With advice such as, "Who cares what the others think? What do you want?" or, "Wow, you really are taking action to live in your purpose! I am so proud of you," and, "When are you going to wake up and stop ignoring the inner call you know you hear? Why are you ignoring it?"

Judgement is the divine companion to evoke when you need to see the highest version of yourself. When you need to connect with the larger consciousness and stop drowning out your inner voice with fearful noise. I know it can be scary, but trust me; when you are ready, be brave and call on Judgement to help you awaken.

Creating Personal Connections

Connecting with Judgement on a personal level happens when you relive moments of self-connection. When you realize you may have been living for others' truths instead of your own. This can happen when you realize you have been working at a job you hate but it's because you don't want to let others down. Or when you go to school for a certain career but realize it isn't your passion.

My real-life connection with Judgement was when I quit my corporate job and decided to be a full-time professional tarot reader. Do you think my mom had that card in the deck when she was planning my future? Definitely not, but my decision wasn't for her. It was for me. I was answering my own inner calling to do what I love and love what I do.

What is your "quit your corporate job" moment? When can you recall listening to your inner voice telling you that you had to change your life path?

Reversal Prompt Questions

How can you release the mindset of self-doubt?

What is blocking you from being able to forgive those who have harmed you?

Why are you resisting listening to your inner calling?

21 The World

The Magician is not truly a master until he is the World.

You have done it! Met all the personas of the Major Arcana as you stand in the presence of completion. The World is the last persona of the Major Arcana as they are the end incarnated. They bring victorious closure, as you can see from the completed wreath that encompasses them. Around them, you see the familiar faces of the divine guardians of the zodiac that were shown in the Wheel of Fortune, but this time without their wings. The World may be connected to the sky, but their energies can be felt here on earth. They bring you the energies of successful endings. With two wands in their hands, you can see they are the master of both worlds: the heavens and the earth. They are the union of the subconscious and conscious.

Does the blue background of the clear sky fill you with bliss and clarity? Can you feel yourself resting after a successful journey of meeting twenty-two new confidants? Do you feel abundant with so many new relationships built? If the answer is yes, then you, my friend, have tapped into the World, and they may have even brought you to the end of an old cycle, opening you up to an entirely new future.

Talking to the World in a Reading

How can you welcome the end when it can feel so bittersweet? When the World steps forward, they do so with advice rooted in a cycle well completed. No, this isn't an undoing of what no longer serves you or a rebirth born from an awakening. This is an ending that provides you with the feelings of closure and fulfillment. You have worked hard to get to this ending, which should feel like an accompaniment. When the World comes forward, they do so with advice such as, "You have worked so hard! Now it's time to rest and release," or, "This time in your life has come to an end. You've done all you were meant to do," and, "Allow yourself to be open to success; you've earned it! Now allow yourself to take it all in."

The World is who you talk to when you need to look at the areas of your life where, yes, you have been successful, but also it is time to close the curtain.

Creating Personal Connections

I want you to recall a time where, yes, there was an ending, but the overall experience was successful. A modern-day example could be the completion of high school or college. The World can even be seen in a marriage beginning or in some cases ending if the divorce is amicable. The World is seen every time a small business is created, or a book is written.

What is your experience with the World? If you are having a hard time, just think of what you are doing right now. You have completed connecting with the Major Arcana. The cycle has ended, and you were successful in completing it. Now it's time to enter a new journey—the one where you will meet the personas of the Minor Arcana and connect with them.

Rest if you need to and then open yourself up to the new beginning.

Reversal Prompt Questions

Why are you resisting the end?

What is blocking you from embracing closure?

How can you release control and allow yourself inner fulfillment?

Chapter Three
The Suit of Pentacles

The suit of earth and everything that grows from its fertile grounds.

The pentacles are one of the most adored suits in the Minor Arcana because they are closely connected to earthly riches. This is not a wrong connection to make, as the pentacles can absolutely bring messages of money, but the way I have learned to truly resonate with them beyond their monetary associations is to understand that the pentacles deal with all things that root us in the physical world, such as our homelife, our health, and our career endeavors.

The pentacles speak to us in a practical way and give advice on working hard toward reaching tangible goals. They show up in everyday moments like working on a team project at work or experiencing a bad health week where everyone in the house seems to be passing around the same cold.

Connecting with the personas of the pentacles means to connect with moments that show up every day outside of you. Moments where something can be created, achieved, gained, or felt in the physical world.

Ace of Pentacles

The aces are the personas of new beginnings, presenting opportunities for you to seize. With the Ace of Pentacles, accepting their gift promises you tangible earthly rewards.

You are meeting the Ace of Pentacles in the garden of unlimited potential. They are holding a large golden coin with a pentacle drawn in the center. Their hand does not point down but upward as if handing you this golden opportunity. There are no human figures shown, but instead, clouds surround this giant hand, symbolizing this gift being given from the heavens. If you look around, all you can see are signs of good health and abundance. The gate in the background is open, letting you know that the Ace of Pentacles brings an opening into your life if you were to follow the yellow path that illuminates before you.

Will you accept this gift from the universe?

Talking to the Ace of Pentacles in Conversation

When the Ace of Pentacles steps forward, they create an opening in the conversation. An opening for future prosperity, opportunity, and rewards. They are rooted in all things beginning and manifesting in the physical world, and because of this, that is where their advice will stem from. They will say things such as, "If you can see this as a new opportunity, what will you make of it?" or, "It's time to begin something new; what skill set can you nurture now that will reward you in the future?" and, "There is potential for tangible manifestation right now; how can you harness this opportunity?"

The Ace of Pentacles is the perfect companion when you are looking for the best place to plant a seed for the future. Call upon them when you need to see what opportunities are available to you and how you can use these openings for future abundance.

Creating a Personal Connection

Have you ever received a small check in the mail and thought, "Where did this come from?" That is a real-life experience with the Ace of Pentacles. They don't always show up in a loud way; that's not really the Minor Arcana's style. They tend to be quieter energies that can build momentum over time.

One of my favorite experiences with the Ace of Pentacles was when I met the lovely acquisitions editor for this very book. She walked into the metaphysical store I was working at one random day, and we struck up a friendly conversation. I shared with her the idea of writing this book, and she smiled while handing me her card. It would be about a year before I reached out to her, but when I did, the opening created that day would soon bloom into rewards.

It was an everyday moment that created an opening for future opportunities. I didn't have to work for it or even plan it. It was a gift from the universe. Think of a time in your life when something just fell into place and created a beginning for you. Was it when your boss walked in and said they randomly put your name in the ring for a new position with better opportunities? Or when you put in an offer on a house that you weren't quite sure you would get, but somehow the owners accepted your offer?

What experience comes to mind where things just lined up so perfectly and created almost a domino effect of rewards?

Reversal Prompt Questions

What is a block that you are currently facing when it comes to allowing financial prosperity into your life?

How can you release the fear you have of success?

What resistance do you have to starting healthy habits in your life?

Two of Pentacles

The professional juggler of the Minor Arcana; the Two of Pentacles balances life's demands with adaptability and harmony.

You are meeting the Two of Pentacles right in the middle of their balancing act. You see them juggling their two coins perfectly as if they have figured out the secret to perfect harmony. The golden infinity symbol shines brightly, representing that they are in flow with the universe itself. With their clothes in the bold colors of red and orange, they are confident in their skills and are powerful enough to keep up their act indefinitely. As you look behind them, you see two boats riding the waves of life's everyday ups and downs. This does not distract the juggler, however. They face you, symbolizing their ability to focus and adapt to all situations.

Talking to the Two of Pentacles in Conversation

When someone as good at multitasking as the Two of Pentacles comes forward, they do so with advice rooted in unwavering balance. They have been learning to prioritize for a long time and will recommend that you do the same. Their advice will sound like, "You know you can't handle it all, so pick what's really important for you to prioritize," or, "How can you be more flexible in this situation?" and maybe even, "How can you stay grounded right now while things are in flux?"

The Two of Pentacles is the persona of handling what life gives you with grace and knowing what you can juggle and what you can't. Because of this, it's best to call on them when you feel you have too many balls in the air and need help prioritizing.

Creating a Personal Connection

With today's number of expectations being placed upon the shoulders of one single person, it isn't hard to relate to the Two of Pentacles.

What experiences have you had lately where you had to find a creative way to maintain balance in your life? Was it creating a daily routine that allowed your body and mind to be in harmony? Was it downloading an app that allowed you to write down all your tasks and set a priority level for each? Either way, think of examples where you needed to multitask but also remind yourself that you can only handle so much at once.

Reversal Prompt Questions

Where do you see resistance within yourself when it comes to setting boundaries with your time and not taking on too much at once?

Why do you have a block when it comes to accepting change and going with the flow?

How can you release the mindset that financial balance is impossible?

Three of Pentacles

Crafting with skill and teamwork, I introduce you to the dream team of collaboration: the Three of Pentacles.

You are meeting the incarnated saying, "Teamwork makes the dream work." As you can see, you are not meeting them when they are done with their life's work but when they are right in the middle of crafting it. If you look at all three of them, you can tell they come from different backgrounds, have different skills, and see from different perspectives, yet they all work together successfully. They aren't crafting something that will be short-lived; no, they are working with stone. They are building the foundation of something that will last generations.

Talking to the Three of Pentacles in Conversation

Three may be a crowd to some, but when you need advice on successfully building your future, you want the Three of Pentacles to chime in on the conversation. They are all about healthy collaborations and being able to work together as a unit to create something larger than yourself. Because of this, their advice in a reading will sound like, "If you are only seeing from your perspective, you are missing the bigger picture," or, "Who can you invite into this situation to help you grow?" and, "What is your role when it comes to working with others? Are you truly being a team player?"

The Three of Pentacles invites you to step out of "me" energy and into the "we."

Creating a Personal Connection

We've all been asked to work with others. Some of us are happy to collaborate, others not so much. When you are looking to connect a personal experience to the Three of Pentacles, look back at when being part of a team or organization actually benefited you.

Was it when you were starting your business and had to work with not only a financial lender but also an accountant? I would say those are some crucial members of your team right there. Was it when you were paired up with some other students in class and had to work together to complete a project worth a large portion of your grade? Or when you decided to start a social media account and needed a team of not only social media experts but marketing and content creation professionals as well?

Think about moments when you knew you had to reach out to others to achieve your goals. Those are the moments where the Three of Pentacles can be seen.

Reversal Prompt Questions

Why do you have resistance toward working with others? Is it a control issue or a trust issue?

How can you release the mindset that only *you* can achieve your goals? Why can't you let others help you?

What is blocking you from seeing the larger picture? Why can you only see from your perspective?

Four of Pentacles

The king who held on so tightly to anything, closed himself off from everything.

The Four of Pentacles is the king of security, possessiveness, and caution when it comes to the material world. How do I know this? Well, look at him. He is so scared to lose all he has gained that he holds on to it tightly with both hands, nestling it in his chest, blocking his heart entirely. His feet rest on the two coins beneath him, letting you know his stability is based on what he has accumulated. The coin above his head symbolizes the repercussions of his fear as it blocks his connection to the heavens above. He may have what others would view as a lot of wealth, but what is he doing with it? Nothing. He is holding it, scared he will never have this much again. This, my friends, is what we call a scarcity mindset, and man, the Four of Pentacles suffers from it. If you look in the background, you can see his kingdom is abundant, healthy, and stable, but he cannot even face it. He faces forward, worrying about the future, trying to hold on tightly to the present. He is completely closing himself off from the world he worked so hard to build, unable to open himself up to its stability and abundance.

Talking to the Four of Pentacles in Conversation

When the Four of Pentacles decides to come forward and speak with you, then you know the advice is going to be rooted in a place of caution. He can't help it; it's who he is. He is going to advise you to be wise with your current assets and recommend you make a financial plan. He is a man who holds on tightly to what he has so he's going to advise you to do the same, even if it's not what's best for you. Now, I am not saying his wisdom should be ignored—no way! What I am saying is there is a way to have a healthy relationship with the material world without clinging too tightly to it. The Four of Pentacles may give you advice such as, "Do you have a plan for the future? You never know what could happen," or, "Make sure you aren't investing everything you have; everyone needs a nest egg," and, "Right now you are being a little careless; try to calm down and ground before you get too carried away."

We all need a little grounding from time to time. That's where the Four of Pentacles comes in. He is the perfect person to call upon when you need a little reminder to save what you have and track what you're spending. He doesn't mean to ruin the party; he just doesn't want you to lose what you have worked so hard for. This is great advice, and we love him for it, but also don't go to the extreme and feel like you have to worry all the time about money. Don't block your blessings.

Creating a Personal Connection

I will be honest: the Four of Pentacles and I are frenemies. I respect his commitment to managing his money but sometimes he pops up right when I am trying to self-soothe with a little treat. Rude! Am I right?

The Four of Pentacles is the master of his money, so when you have moments of, "Hey, I really need to create a budget," or, "Let me sit down and go over my bank statements," you are speaking his language. In those moments, you are aligning with the positive characteristics of this persona.

But in the moments when you are scared to splurge a little on a loved one or even yourself for fear of never seeing a return, you are aligning with his more negative traits. Holding on so tightly to what you have can block you from what you could receive if you just loosened up a little.

It's okay to invest in your success.

Reversal Prompt Questions

Why do you resist releasing some control over your finances?

What is blocking you from being more structured when it comes to your financial life, homelife, and so on?

How can you release yourself from a scarcity mindset?

Five of Pentacles

To meet poverty in all aspects of life is to meet the Five of Pentacles.

Poor in health and poor in wealth, the Five of Pentacles is the persona of earthly struggle and resilience. As you can see, the Five of Pentacles could be doing better. They are outside in the dead of winter with no shelter, no food, and no one to help. I would say they are hopeless, but that would not be the truth. As you can see, one of the figures looks up at the warm bright lights from the church window as if showing you how much hope they still have. This is a sad point in their lives for you to meet them, but it is not without a light at the end of the tunnel. The Five of Pentacles does not struggle alone. There are two figures that make up this persona. They are in this together, body and soul.

Talking to the Five of Pentacles in Conversation

No one wants advice on struggling, but if you must listen to anyone, I recommend you listen to the Five of Pentacles. They have been there and know what overcoming a difficult period in life is like. So, when they come forward, it is with advice rooted in the moment you meet them. They will ask you questions such as, "What actions can you take to overcome this difficult time in your life?" or, "Yes, right now it is difficult, but that doesn't mean you just give up," and, "You are not alone in your suffering, remember that others are affected by this as well."

The Five of Pentacles may be the last persona you want to see, but when you are going through a difficult time and need hope for the future, they just might be the perfect companion to help you shift your mindset.

Creating a Personal Connection

I feel like recalling a painful time in your life may come to you quickly, so I will keep this part short. Just know that you will find the Five of Pentacles in moments where you felt as though all was lost, only to have found a way out. Moments where you lost your job and had to struggle for a while but were eventually able to find another. Or moments when you were battling some health issues with recovery being slow and painful. Those are moments when the Five of Pentacles can be found.

My first time meeting the Five of Pentacles was when I was eighteen trying to live in my own apartment. I was working a retail job that paid minimum wage and was as irresponsible with money as one could be. This caused me to create a world of struggle for not only myself but for my roommate as well. We were both terrible with money, if I am being honest, so having the lights or water turned off was just an average day for us. Eating dollar hotdogs from a gas station and using restaurant toilet paper, we were absolutely living a life that reflected the Five of Pentacles.

Can you recall a time in your life that has the same energies of poor health in all worldly things?

Reversal Prompt Questions

What mental block is preventing you from believing your situation will get better?

How can you release yourself from past struggles and embrace your new, improved life?

Why is there resistance when it comes to accepting your secured finances? Why are you still carrying the hardships?

Six of Pentacles

Charity does have a name, and that name is the Six of Pentacles.

We love a person who is genuinely giving, and that, my friend, is exactly who the Six of Pentacles is. The persona of personal generosity, sharing of abundance, and giver of gifts. They are the best friend who picks up the tab at a restaurant or spends their time helping you move without asking for anything in return. Looking at them, you can see one figure who is quite wealthy, resembling a noble, sharing their financial abundance with the two figures below. It should be noted that the wealthy noble does hold a scale in his hand as he knows exactly how much to give without giving too much. This is important to note because we are all guilty of giving too much of ourselves to those around us. The Six of Pentacles does not do this as they are generous of course but also balanced.

Talking to the Six of Pentacles in Conversation

When the giver comes up in conversation, it is a gift in itself. The Six of Pentacles is the most generous persona in the Minor Arcana, so when they step forward, it is to either be generous or encourage you to be. Their advice is rooted in their gifting nature, so when you speak to them, you will hear things such as, "How are you supporting yourself and those around you?" or, "Do you have something you could share with others? It doesn't have to be money, but think about what you are abundant in right now," and, "How open are you to accepting help? Are you allowing others who love you to show you support?"

The Six of Pentacles may ask you to give, but they can also ask you to receive, so call them forward when you need to see where future support lies. They are a good go-to persona when you need to know where your generosity is best spent. It's one thing to be generous to those who need it but another to be taken advantage of by those who don't.

Creating a Personal Connection

In this world, time is money, and everyone has less and less of both. The Six of Pentacles shows up in moments where, even with the state of the world, there is the energy of sharing. This can look like sharing your time with others or donating your clothes to a local shelter. This can even look like accepting support from another, even though it's hard for you to receive.

One of my most beloved moments where I connected with the Six of Pentacles was when I was first getting to know my husband, and he showed up on my doorstep with groceries. At the time, we were just friends, but he knew I was struggling financially and still living off those dollar hot dogs from the gas station. I didn't have to ask him for help; I mean, to be honest, he knew I would never. My Capricorn rising and Taurus moon wouldn't allow it. So, what did he do? He went to the grocery store, bought items he thought I would like, and just quietly left them on my doorstep. He didn't need praise or thanks; he just did it because that's the type of person he is. I will never forget that moment. That is a moment that speaks to the charitable energy that is the Six of Pentacles.

Can you recall a time when you were charitable to another or allowed yourself to receive charity?

Reversal Prompt Questions

Why are you resisting allowing others to help you?

What is blocking you from stopping the pattern of giving too much?

How can you release the attachment to this unequal situation?

Seven of Pentacles

With patience and vision, the Seven of Pentacles is the persona of long-term growth and effort.

You are meeting the dedicated gardener of the Minor Arcana. If you look at their expression, they appear indifferent toward their crop, even though it is beginning to turn green and luscious. Some areas still need attention clearly, but if you look closely, one coin of reward has already fallen from the vine. From the looks of it, the Seven of Pentacles was hoping more rewards would be yielded by this time, but he will not give up. He knows there is much to be gained if one only has the patience to wait.

Talking to the Seven of Pentacles in Conversation

Talking to the Seven of Pentacles is talking to patience personified. They know that it takes hard work, persistence, and patience to see rewards. Because of this mindset, their advice will sound like, "Why the rush? This needs time to grow," or, "This isn't something that will happen overnight. You need to continue to nurture this before you see any rewards," and, "Every season for every reason, it's not time yet. You will know when the time is right."

When you feel like you are getting frustrated and ready to give up, ask the Seven of Pentacles to ground you and remind you that some things cannot be rushed. They will show you the best areas in your life to focus on and what situations will reap rewards after some long-term nourishment.

Creating a Personal Connection

Patience is a virtue, but man can it be annoying! Sometimes you just have to wait to see the fruits of your labor, you know? Can you think of a time in your life when that statement rings true? When did you have to dedicate not only time but patience to a certain experience before you saw results? College always comes up as an example for me when I am connecting with the Seven of Pentacles. It takes four years of patient dedication to finally receive that degree.

What is your college? What have you gone through that took patience and dedication?

Reversal Prompt Questions

What is blocking you from being patient with yourself and your work? Why do you need to rush this process?

How can you release yourself from the attachment to a certain outcome?

Why are you resistant to continuing to work even if it isn't going to plan?

Eight of Pentacles

The master of diligence and focus, the Eight of Pentacles perfects his craft through dedication.

You are meeting him right as he hammers away at his latest creation. Clearly it isn't his final masterpiece, or he wouldn't still be working on it, but as you can see from the other coins around him, he has been working tirelessly to create what he feels is the perfect piece. Each coin is a reflection of his pursuit toward excellence, embodying his commitment to personal improvement. He wears red stockings of power and confidence as his blue shirt of peace is covered by a protective craftsman's apron. Looking in the background, you see he is outside of his home. He is at work, in his shop, using his tools of creation, not unlike the Magician. His face does not show displeasure but dedication to the journey of mastery; the Eight of Pentacles knows that with each stroke of his hammer, he is one step closer to perfection.

Talking to the Eight of Pentacles in Conversation

When this ambitious persona comes forward, you know they arrive with expert advice. They are rooted in commitment and will provide advice such as, "You know that practice makes perfect; don't give up so easily," or, "A little extra training never hurt anyone; can you learn more about this subject?" and, "It may seem boring on the surface, but how can you go deeper and find enjoyment?"

You will want to talk to the Eight of Pentacles when you need someone to show you where you can achieve mastery. Where your natural talent resides, as well as where you may be trying a little too hard to achieve perfection.

Creating a Personal Connection

What is the difference between dedication and devotion? There really isn't one when it comes to the Eight of Pentacles.

Think about a time when you had to put in 100 percent and then maybe even more. When I think about my personal experience with the Eight of Pentacles, I think about when I first picked up reading the tarot. Learning the meanings, forming connections with the cards, and interpreting different spreads didn't just happen overnight. It took years of consistent dedication to my practice to get where I am today, and guess what? I see no end in sight.

What moment is coming forward for you? Was it when you had to take an internship in your field of study or when you had to watch training courses before you started your new job? These are all moments where you will find the Eight of Pentacles. Where do they show up in your life?

Reversal Prompt Questions

What is blocking your motivation to keep trying?

How can you release the resistance you have to hard work?

Why are you resisting becoming a professional? Do you have a fear of success or authority?

Nine of Pentacles

Self-sufficient and opulent, the Nine of Pentacles basks in her success and comfort.

Welcome to the garden of all things hard-earned and now enjoyed. This is where you meet the Nine of Pentacles in all her luxury. She wears a golden dress ordained with abundant flowers from head to toe. Her head covering and sleeves are red with confidence and self-empowerment. The landscape behind her is flourishing and fertile, while the sky is yellow with radiating joy. You see a falcon resting on her hand, symbolizing that she didn't just stumble upon this success; it was self-made with dedication and hard work.

She is the embodiment of achieved success in this earthly world.

Talking to the Nine of Pentacles in Conversation

When you need a motivator to keep up the excellent work, there is no better reminder of rewards earned than the Nine of Pentacles. She is rooted in her achievements and all they have brought her; because of this, her advice will sound like, "There is success that can be felt when one believes in their own abilities and strengthens those abilities," or, "Take time to visualize what success looks like to you. Now what actions do you need to take to make this image a reality?" and, "You have done it! You have worked so hard! Now is the time to enjoy all that you have achieved through those personal sacrifices!"

Find the Nine of Pentacles when you need a reminder to treat yourself or when you need to step into a gratitude mindset. She is the perfect persona to show you what success looks like to you and what steps you need to take to achieve it. She is also a great reminder that everyone needs a little luxury in their lives; it's okay to spoil yourself every now and again.

Creating a Personal Connection

When was the last time you felt abundant? It doesn't have to be abundant in money. It could be abundant in love, health, friendships, and so on. What about a time when you spoiled yourself a little? Gave yourself a little spa day or bought an outfit you had your eye on? Maybe even splurged and got new bedding that made your bed feel like a cloud?

These are all moments when you can feel the Nine of Pentacles. The moments where you enjoy the fruits of your labor and get to live in your hard-earned success.

Reversal Prompt Questions

What is blocking you from being independent? Why do you allow yourself to rely on others?

How can you release the mindset that success is rooted in evil? How can you reframe this thought process?

Why are you resistant to splurging a little on yourself?

Ten of Pentacles

Rooted in legacy and wealth, the Ten of Pentacles is the persona of family, ancestry, and security.

If this card feels a little overwhelming to you, don't worry; there is a lot going on here. If you look at only the figures on the card, you can see that this family is multigenerational. We have a young married couple and their child, as well as an elderly man resting alongside his animal companions, symbols of loyalty and honor. The elderly man is the representation of generational wealth as well as the connection to the family members who are no longer earthside. There is a divine connection here, an ancestral one. Looking at the young couple and their child, you can see that the legacy of this family will live on. It is alive and well, as is its influence.

As you look around, you see stone structures everywhere. This speaks to the stability of this family as well as how long they have been here. They are not building these structures; the foundations are solid, the community is established, and so is this family. They aren't going anywhere—well, not anytime soon.

Talking to the Ten of Pentacles in Conversation

The Ten of Pentacles is the persona of a strong, stable, and wealthy family, so when they step forward, they do so rooted in family values. They will come forward with advice of, "How have you secured your assets for the future?" or, "How can you support your family right now? Or are you the one who needs support?" and, "Do you have any type of relationship with your ancestors? How can you honor them?"

Call the Ten of Pentacles when you need to see the wealth that surrounds you or when you need to find the path that will help you build generational wealth and financial stability.

Creating a Personal Connection

How you define wealth will really impact how you connect with this card. For the longest time, I did not consider my family wealthy. We were middle-class, living paycheck to paycheck, and putting every vacation on credit cards. This didn't scream wealth to me. But that is because I was looking at it from my own point of view, not a worldly point of view. Once I took off my "growing up in the suburbs" glasses, I could see how wealthy we really were. I didn't have to struggle to find food. My clothes were clean and mostly new. My bed was comfortable and covered in blankets galore. I didn't need or want for anything. I was wealthy, and so was my family. I was living the Ten of Pentacles.

I give you this example, so you don't look for extravagant examples when you are trying to connect with the Ten of Pentacles. Think of moments when your family was stable, financially secure, and acting as a unit.

That is where you will find the Ten of Pentacles.

Reversal Prompt Questions

What is blocking you and your family from working together as one?

How can you release the mindset of insecurity?

Why is there resistance to resolving your family conflict?

Page of Pentacles

The persona of curiosity and eagerness for learning, the Page of Pentacles is ready to explore all the opportunities they can hold.

The Page of Pentacles is the youthful student who is just starting out on their journey. We know this is a new beginning; as you can see, they only hold one coin in their hand, looking at it with optimism and determination. Their clothes are as green as they are. Standing in front of a bright sunny day, the landscape around them is green with fertile possibilities but not overgrown with accomplishments as the seeds are just now being planted. You see a mountain in the far distance, letting you know this will be an uphill battle. The Page of Pentacles doesn't let that stop them, though; they face forward, planning their future and its inevitable rewards.

Talking to the Page of Pentacles in Conversation

When the student comes forward, the intelligent observer sees a master in the making.

I say this so you know not to dismiss the Page of Pentacles when they step forward to speak with you. Yes, they can represent someone in your life, but if that makes them difficult to form a connection with, I want you to focus on their characteristics instead. The Page of Pentacles is practical, disciplined, and studious. These are the roots from which their advice will grow. So, they may give advice such as, "This is a great time to start something new; embrace being a student again," and, "Now is a great time to begin a new healthy lifestyle," or, "You are just starting out, so make sure you stay dedicated to your future goals."

The Page of Pentacles is the perfect persona to speak with when you have the feeling that it's time to start from the bottom up. When you are ready to dedicate time and patience to a new project that will reward you in the future, the Page of Pentacles is good with their resources and will remind you to be the same.

Creating a Personal Connection

Because the page is a court card, I would be negligent if I didn't invite you to at least try to think about someone in your life who reminds you of them. The court cards do have a traditional association with people in our lives, so I will take this opportunity to invite you to form a personal connection in this way. Who is a student in your life right now? Who may be focused on planning their financial future or creating new healthy habits?

If you have someone in mind who resonates with these characteristics, then you are connecting with the Page of Pentacles. If you can't think of someone, I want you to think of moments in your life when you have embodied these energies. When were you a student in a new profession? When did you receive an opportunity for future investment? What was a time in your life that required you to commit and get serious?

These are all also moments when you embodied the Page of Pentacles.

Reversal Prompt Questions

What is blocking you from being committed?

Why are you resistant to beginnings?

How can you release your current mindset that is keeping you stagnant?

Knight of Pentacles

A reliable and persistent persona, the Knight of Pentacles rides forward with diligent care.

One of the most honest and trustworthy personas of the Minor Arcana, the Knight of Pentacles looks like your classic knight in shiny armor. However, they are not in action at the time of your meeting. They are in a moment of pause, weighing their options before crossing the river. Their black stallion, with greenery sprouting from its head, represents the knight's slow growth and future potential. They hold their coin responsibly, looking at it with committed eyes. They know what they want to achieve will take time and feel there is no need to rush the journey.

Talking to the Knight of Pentacles in Conversation

When the Knight of Pentacles slowly rolls in to the conversation, then you know whatever you are working toward is going to take time. The Knight of Pentacles is patient, so remember that when they give you advice such as, "What are some steps you can take right now to slowly grow your finances?" or, "How much of your time are you willing to commit to making this successful?" and even, "It won't happen overnight, but it will happen if you stay dedicated and keep moving forward."

The Knight of Pentacles is dependable, hardworking, and practical. Call on them when you need to see in what area of your life you need these energies. Where can commitment and self-determination benefit you?

Creating a Personal Connection

We all know someone who takes it one step at a time. They do not rush into action or create a scene; they think about all the possibilities and then make their choice. It's usually a great choice, too. That is who the Knight of Pentacles will reflect as someone in your life. They will be trustworthy, calm, and maybe even a little cautious with what they have. They aren't in a hurry, which can sometimes be frustrating when you are ready to take the next step.

If this sounds like you or someone you know, then yay! You already have a personal connection, but if you are still struggling, think about a time in your life when you just had to take it slow. It may have been annoying to do so, but you knew that to succeed, you couldn't rush things.

When I think about the Knight of Pentacles, I think about the steps it took to write this book for you. It was a slow and steady process that I knew would yield rewards. What is a project you have undertaken that you knew would take a while before it would be completed? Maybe studying to be a doctor or nurse? Maybe becoming a painter and having to learn about color theory and art history? There are so many moments in our lives that require slow, dedicated effort; what is yours?

Reversal Prompt Questions

Why do you feel resistant to patience when it comes to building your future?

What is blocking you from continuing to commit to your goals?

How can you release expectations when it comes to what you are trying to manifest?

Queen of Pentacles

Who is this abundant woman who bears a striking resemblance to the Empress? That would be the Queen of Pentacles, and believe me, she is just as loving.

Just like with the Empress, you are meeting the Queen of Pentacles in her overgrown garden of health and fertility. She has earned her place on the throne by being responsible and caring with the resources she holds. Her coin carefully sits in her lap as she looks at it with loving and nurturing eyes. She is a mother, after all. Nurturing and loving the world around her is how she grew such an abundant landscape filled with flowers in the first place. She is a grounded queen, as you can see. She sits between two mountains perfectly in the middle, in balance, as her feet touch the earth beneath her. This does not mean she is an emotionless ruler; you can see there is a healthy stream in the background. She has emotions, she just doesn't let them overwhelm her.

She is the embodiment of earthly health, wealth, and love.

Talking to the Queen of Pentacles in Conversation

When the queen of the earthly kingdom steps forward, you know her advice will come from a mother's heart. This doesn't mean she will always represent a mother but that she is rooted in the characteristics of one. She is nurturing, caring, dependable, responsible, and loving. So, her advice will sound like, "When was the last time you focused on yourself and building your own future rather than someone else's?" or, "You are the one that grows your life; how can you affirm this confidence in yourself?" and, "It's time to look at your own assets; how can you take control of your finances?"

The Queen of Pentacles is the ruler of her world. She doesn't need someone to do things for her. Call her forward when you need to see where in your life you could give yourself more authority. The areas in your life that are ready to heal and grow by you pouring love into them.

What areas of your life need you to be a confident and caring mother? That is what the Queen of Pentacles will show you.

Creating a Personal Connection

Who is the empowered provider in your life right now? Think of someone who is independent, great with money, lives a life of luxury and is healthy mentally and physically. If someone is coming forward, then you have yourself a real-life Queen of Pentacles. Even if you know someone who is maybe two out of the four above characteristics, you still might know a Queen of Pentacles. She can even show up as a mother or friend in your life, but one who is patient and kind instead of overly financially wealthy. There is more than one form of wealth in this world.

If you don't know anyone like this, think about a time when you had to focus on your own growth instead of investing in others. The Queen of Pentacles shows up in your life in the moments when you have to care about yourself and take some time for your own glow-up. This can look like taking a step back from working for someone else's company and starting your own, or creating a healthy routine that will allow you to be physically, mentally, and spiritually fulfilled. Or even creating a budget, opening your own bank account, and starting a rainy-day fund.

These are all moments where the Queen of Pentacles is present. What is coming forward for you right now?

Reversal Prompt Questions

What is blocking you from being connected to your body right now?

How can you release the mindset that to have money is to be greedy with money?

Why are you resistant to breaking the patterns that are keeping you from being financially secure?

King of Pentacles

If you love healthy, secure, wealthy, and trustworthy masculine energy, then let me introduce you to the King of Pentacles. The King of Pentacles is the personification of success. He is honest, hardworking, protective, and generous. How do I know this? Let's look at where you are meeting him.

As you can see from all the abundance around him, he doesn't want for anything. He has worked hard and achieved everything he set his mind to. His throne is abundant with healthy greenery, showing just how fertile he is. His clothes are ordained with sweet grapes as their vines grow prosperously behind him. You see his protective nature poking out by looking at his feet and catching a glimpse of his suit of armor. He holds his coin of all things earned in one hand as a golden scepter stands straight in the other. The kingdom that he provides for sits proudly in the background. Look at how strong and stable those buildings are—symbols of his strength as a leader and how successful he is at seeing the long-term vision.

Talking to the King of Pentacles in Conversation

It's always nice to speak with someone who can give you advice on how to be successful because they are themselves. That is where the King of Pentacles's advice will always stem from: success. He is the embodiment of it, so his advice will sound like, "How can you commit to your own success at this moment?" or, "What healthy habits can you root yourself in right now in order to grow?" and, "Is there someone in your life you can go to for some financial mentorship? Are you that person?"

Find the King of Pentacles when you need to see where you are already successful in your life or when you need him to show you the path to future financial rewards and material stability. He knows you have it in you; all you have to do is let him show you.

Creating a Personal Connection

I feel like we all, at some point in our lives, try to manifest a wealthy benefactor—am I right? No? Just me and my Capricorn rising?

If you have, then know you aren't alone in this manifestation. The King of Pentacles shows up in people we know who are generous with their time and money. People who have built successful business empires and will happily show you how they did it. People who give great financial advice because they still use a check register log and know exactly how much money is going in and out of their accounts.

They can also show up as people in your life who are just great at achieving long-term goals or someone who loves to be part of their local community. Every time I see the King of Pentacles, I can't help but think of my husband because he is not only great at finances, but he is one of those rare adults in my life who can actually save for a long-term goal. Not me, though. I am a "check the bank account as I go" girl, and if my credit card has an available balance, then you can count on me to get that little treat.

If you find yourself struggling to connect with the King of Pentacles as a person in your life, then remember that he can also show up as lived experiences. That time when you bought a piggy bank and actually started putting money in it. Or when you went to secure financing from the bank for your business. The time when you paid off all your credit cards and still had a savings account. Even a time when, out of the kindness of your heart, you gave either time or money to someone who needed help.

You will find the King of Pentacles in all these experiences. Where does he show up in your life?

Reversal Prompt Questions

How can you release the mindset that you always know what's best?

What is blocking you from creating a budget or savings account?

Why do you have resistance when it comes to going with the flow? Why do you feel the need to always be in control?

Chapter Four
The Suit of Wands

The suit of fire and everything that is fueled by it.

From creative projects, spiritual awakenings, expansive travels, and passionate relationships, the fire of the wands suit can be felt from the inside out.

Think of the wands as the energy that propels you forward in life. They spark you to start something new and embrace change with enthusiasm. They are the actions you take and the momentum needed to keep going. From staying motivated to keep working hard toward that promotion to going on that dream vacation to an exotic place. The wands show up to remind you that you have the spark within to create a soul-led life.

Ace of Wands

When the universe hands you the gift of awakening to life, you may call it the Ace of Wands.

You are meeting the personification of all things newly inspired. This can be new ideas, passions, spiritual identities, and even desires. As you look at the hand from the divine, you see it holding a large wand. This wand stands out against the grey-neutral background with what looks like the beginning stages of an abundant landscape. The wand is not overgrown with greenery but seems to have a few branches beginning to sprout.

This is the gift of divine spark. How will you use it to create change in your life?

Talking to the Ace of Wands in Conversation

You know things are about to get a burst of energy when the Ace of Wands comes forward to talk. They are rooted in their energetic new beginnings, so their advice may sound like, "This is your chance to pursue that exciting idea you've been dreaming about," or, "Harness this surge of enthusiasm to kickstart a new project," and, "Hello, passion! Where can I channel this newfound drive to bring about positive change?"

It's always a good idea to welcome in the fiery energy of new beginnings in your life. So, bring the Ace of Wands forward when you need help not only feeling energized but also seeing where that new energy can birth something in your life.

Creating a Personal Connection

When people say they just felt a spark, well, then they are connecting with the Ace of Wands perfectly. Can you remember a time in your life when you just suddenly felt passionate about a project, a person, or a belief system? When you could feel the fire inside of you growing, and you harnessed it to create something tangible?

Those moments are perfect examples of the Ace of Wands.

Reversal Prompt Questions

What is blocking your creativity?

How can you release the patterns of laziness?

Why are you resisting seeing your true potential?

Two of Wands

With the world in their hands, the Two of Wands sits there patiently planning their next adventure.

You are meeting a persona who thinks about all the details before making a decision. As you look at the figure, you can see they stand at the top of their castlelike home, looking out toward their potential future. One hand holds the world while the other rests on a wand of curious exploration. The figure stands between two wands, one connected to his stable home, representing how secure and accomplished he already is, while the other sits high above, next to the world.

Does the figure dare to take the leap and travel into the unknown? He doesn't know yet. He hasn't made his choice.

Talking to the Two of Wands in Conversation

When the Two of Wands comes forward, they do so rooted in their need for a plan. Because of this, their advice will sound like, "Have you thought of all the details?" or, "Before you make a decision, think about all you currently have," and, "There is no need to rush; take a moment to prepare for the next step."

You will find that the Two of Wands will come forward in times of stillness before a bold choice is to be made. Use this as an opportunity to see where a little planning will go a long way when choosing to be adventurous. If you choose to be adventurous, that is.

Creating a Personal Connection

The Two of Wands can be found whenever travel plans are in preparation. This can be when you are first researching a new place and looking up everything you need. Or when you are weighing whether it's even worth it to go. If you have no experience with travel, don't worry; you can also find the Two of Wands in moments when you had to leave your comfort zone. This could be striking a deal with a business partner, moving out of your parents' house, hosting your own art show, filming your first social media video, and so on.

All these experiences took planning as well as guts, and that's exactly what the Two of Wands is all about.

Reversal Prompt Questions

How can you release your fears of the unknown?

What is blocking you from just going all in? Why do you hesitate?

Why do you resist having a plan? Why does it feel constricting to you?

Three of Wands

The ships are setting sail on the seas of ambition, telling the Three of Wands it's time for growth.

You are meeting the persona of personal expansion. Looking at the figure, the first thing you might notice is how bright and yellow the background is. Shining with new opportunities, the figure looks toward the boats in the water. It is time to board and go on a new adventure, but the figure is taking a longer look at the future ahead. The moment of planning has passed; it's time to be courageous and use the energy of all three wands to propel them forward.

Talking to the Three of Wands in Conversation

It's time to branch out, and the perfect persona to guide you is the Three of Wands. They are rooted in their need for personal expansion, so their advice will sound like, "Take this spark and move!" or, "It's time to take real steps toward the future you want. Stop waiting!" and even, "This is an opportunity for real-life travel. Go on that vacation, move to that city, leave that situation."

Connect with the Three of Wands when you need to see the opportunities in your life that will expand you on a soul level. Just make sure once they show you where the openings are, you take the action needed to move toward them.

Creating a Personal Connection

Am I going to suggest you make a connection with the Three of Wands by recalling a period of movement in your life? Yes; yes I am. But the movement could be anything. A literal move, a vacation, a move from one mindset to another, a move into a healthy sexual relationship, a professional move, and so on.

The point is that when movement meets personal growth, you know you have connected with the Three of Wands.

Reversal Prompt Questions

What is blocking you from seeing the growth you have already made?

How can you release the weight of personal regret?

Why are you resistant to facing challenges head-on?

Four of Wands

There are two types of celebration in the tarot: one is the Three of Cups, where we are partying just because we can and should! The other is who you are meeting now, the Four of Wands. They are a little more structured in their celebration as it normally revolves around an event. Known as the personification of marriages, engagements, and rites of passage, the Four of Wands celebrates milestones that bring you home.

Can you tell by all the yellow in the background that you are meeting the Four of Wands during a time of celebrating all things happy? If you look toward the background, you can see two figures raising their hands in celebration as they stand in front of their beautiful family home. Members of their community gather in the distance, showing their support for the figures' milestone. Four wands stand strong and grounded as they are adorned with an abundant victorious wreath filled with the fruits of the figures' labor.

Talking to the Four of Wands in Conversation

When the persona of planned get-togethers comes forward, you know it's about to be a party. They are rooted in the moments of joyful social celebration, so their advice will sound like, "Invite those you love to celebrate all that you have accomplished!" or, "It's time to focus on creating a stable environment, whether at home, work, or within your community. Strong foundations lead to lasting success," and even, "Right now things are going great. Connect with loved ones, take a break, and soak in all the joy that is available to you."

Connect with the Four of Wands when you want to see where life can be a banquet.

Creating a Personal Connection

If your brain instantly went to a memory of a wedding or graduation to connect with the Four of Wands, that is great! The Four of Wands can absolutely represent those moments in our lives. They can also represent a family dinner or a holiday work event. You can find the Four of Wands in moments when you feel secure and content. Or when you feel really grounded in your relationships and or spiritual practice.

Will they show up in planned events? Absolutely! Will they also show up in moments when you just sit back in happiness? You betcha.

Reversal Prompt Questions

What is blocking you from feeling secure in life?

How can you release the mindset that just because an event didn't go as planned means it wasn't successful?

Why are you resistant to celebrating with loved ones?

Five of Wands

Ambitions begin to clash as the persona of conflict and competition, the Five of Wands, comes forward.

As you can see, there are five figures in front of you, all trying to prove themselves. They yield their opposing wands, arguing with one another to the point where no one is actually going to be a winner. The figures are young and immature, arguing for argument's sake. Conflict and personal rivalries fill the air as the tension between the figures seems to be rising.

Talking to the Five of Wands in Conversation

When the persona of disagreements comes forward to offer some advice, you know it's going to stem from a place of conflict. The conflict could be internal or external, but either way, they will sound like, "The struggles you face inside your head will eventually mirror outside in the material world. What can you do to find internal peace?" or, "Things are tense right now; how can you find a compromise?" and, "If you are competing to be seen by others then you have already lost."

You may not want to, but calling on the Five of Wands will help you see where the unnecessary fighting is occurring in your life. This could be in your head where the battle between self-worth and self-sabotage is taking place, or it can be out in the real world in any environment where rivalry is the new camaraderie.

Creating a Personal Connection

When connecting with the Five of Wands, I want you to recall a time when everyone was talking all at once so no one was being heard. This could be when people at work were all trying to impress the boss, and this created an environment of competition. Or when you and your siblings were fighting because that's just what siblings do. Maybe even a moment when you were struggling to get your business off the ground and had to remind yourself of why you were doing it in the first place.

Moments where struggle meets conflict. That is where you will find the Five of Wands.

Reversal Prompt Questions

Why are you so resistant to conflict? Even if it is necessary?

What is blocking you from rising above and working with a team?

How can you release the hold that your ego has over you right now?

Six of Wands

Victory! Victory! We all know your name; it is the Six of Wands we proclaim!

The Six of Wands is the persona of seen success, and if you couldn't tell by looking at them, they are kind of the local celebrity of the tarot. If you look at just the figure alone, you can see they wear a wreath of victory atop their head as a red cape of confidence and courage drapes over them. In their hand, they hold a wand straight to the heavens as it is adorned with its own victory wreath. The horse that carries them is white with purity as it wears a green cape of fertility and abundance. In the background, you can see that the community has come out to publicly celebrate the figure and recognize all they have achieved.

The famous Six of Wands has arrived, and they want you to recognize your own triumphs.

Talking to the Six of Wands in Conversation

It's always nice to speak to someone successful because they can help you recognize the success hiding within you. When the Six of Wands comes forward to talk, just know they are rooted in all things victorious. Because of this, their advice may sound like, "You are the winner! You succeeded, and everyone is going to see it," or, "Enjoy the moment. You worked so hard for this victory. Let people celebrate you," and, "It's all going to work out. Be confident in your abilities and accept praise for them."

When you want to find your path to success, bring the Six of Wands forward and let them show you the way. They can point you in the right direction and help you build confidence in your choices.

Creating a Personal Connection

When was the last time you experienced personal success from past hard work? Was it when you got the highest grade on an exam and were praised by your fellow classmates? Or was it when you got a promotion at work, and they threw you a party?

One of the most memorable moments I had with the Six of Wands was when I received an award at one of my previous employer's holiday parties. They called my name and presented me with a trophy for being, no joke, a ray of sunshine. Everyone clapped and laughed in agreement that I was truly one of the happiest people they had ever worked with. It was my little moment of recognition, and it made me feel like I really had achieved something grand.

Those are the energies that will accompany connecting with the Six of Wands. Being recognized for your efforts and feeling successful because of it. When can you recall feeling this way?

Reversal Prompt Questions

How can you release the mindset that you aren't successful unless others see you as so?

What is blocking you from allowing yourself to feel confident?

Why are you resisting failure? What does it mean to you?

Seven of Wands

Their defenses are up, and they don't plan on backing down anytime soon.

Sometimes you have to stand up for yourself, and that's exactly what the Seven of Wands is doing. You are meeting the persona of self-defense as they are taking a stand against those who try to defeat them. The figure in front of you holds on to their wand of might with both hands, grounding themselves in their beliefs. They won't allow the six wands of challenges below catch them off guard, no way. The background is blue with complete clarity as the landscape shows the figure standing on a hill of higher ground.

The Seven of Wands is the embodiment of remembering that with persistence and strength, any obstacle can be overcome, no matter how many there are.

Talking to the Six of Wands in Conversation

It's time to stand up for yourself, says the Seven of Wands. When this determined persona comes forward in conversation, you know their advice will be rooted in their core values of never backing down. Because of this, their advice will sound like, "Sometimes, in order to achieve what you want, you have to fight for it," or, "Not everyone is going to like what you do, but that doesn't mean you give up," and even, "Do you feel like you're under attack right now? Is life throwing a lot at you? How can you take a second and shift your perspective?"

When things feel a little overwhelming, bring forward the Seven of Wands and let them remind you all that is worth fighting for. They will show you where overcoming life's obstacles will benefit you in the end.

Creating a Personal Connection

When was a moment in your life when you had to stand up for yourself and your choices? Was it when you decided to embrace spirituality and move away from traditional religion or when you chose an unconventional career path? If any of these experiences resonate with you, you have met the Seven of Wands.

You can also find them in moments when you are just doing your best as life throws everything it can at you. Like juggling all the roles you play, such as being a parent, a partner, an employer, and so on.

Connect with the Seven of Wands in moments when you know you won't back down or give up.

Reversal Prompt Questions

How can you release the mindset that you are always under attack?

What is blocking you from standing up for yourself and removing the narrative that you are powerless?

Why are you resisting letting go and letting others win for once?

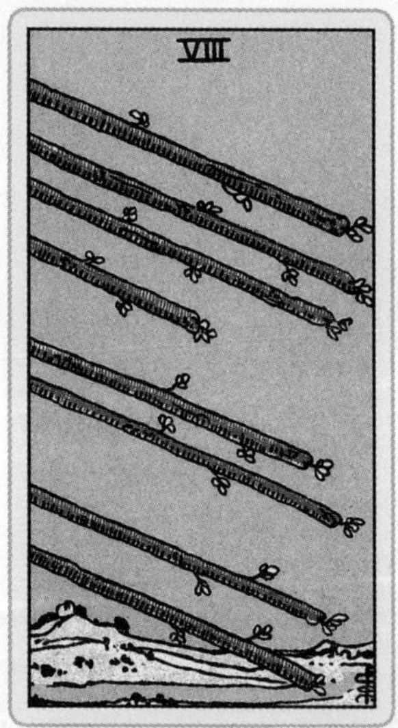

Eight of Wands

The universe is pushing you forward, and when I say universe, I mean the Eight of Wands.

You are meeting the persona of sudden speed, and they don't plan on slowing down anytime soon. As you can see by the eight wands flying through the air, things are progressing quickly, so there is no time for hesitation. Looking at the background, you see no figures or animals, just a blue sky of clarity and eight wands hurtling toward you. In the landscape, there is a faint image of a home and a still river, so things won't stay this energized for long. How are you going to use this divinely gifted momentum to get where you want to be?

Talking to the Eight of Wands in Conversation

Get ready, because when the persona of speed comes to talk, they are doing so with no time to waste on pleasantries. The Eight of Wands only knows one thing: movement. So, when they enter the conversation, it is with advice such as, "Go. Move. Take the very next step needed. Stop waiting," or, "Things are about to pick up; make sure you are ready," and, "Change is unavoidable. Be brave and take control."

When you need help getting motivated or need to see where a change of scenery can help progress your life, call on the Eight of Wands for a quick chat.

Creating a Personal Connection

You know you are connecting with the Eight of Wands when you can feel movement in your life. Sometimes this is movement in the literal sense, such as moving to a new house, going on vacation, traveling for work, and so on. You get what I mean. Other times, it is movement in the sense of life progression. Moving forward on a project that has been in the works for months, moving past personal limitations, progressing quickly in your spiritual practice, picking up speed in a romantic relationship; the list goes on.

Whatever type of movement is coming up for you, allow yourself to feel confident in the fact that you are forming a connection with the Eight of Wands.

Reversal Prompt Questions

How can you release your need for control and just go with the flow?

How can you work through the block when it comes to trusting messages from the universe?

Why do you think you have resistance when it comes to embracing sudden changes?

Nine of Wands

There is no backing down once you have fought tooth and nail to get this far.

You are meeting the persona of perseverance, and as you can see, they have been through it. Looking toward the blue background, you can see in the landscape all the challenges this figure has had to overcome just by the sheer number of mountains behind them. The figure holds their wand of strength close to them as if leaning on it in hopes of gaining the energy for one last stand. They wear no armor of protection but instead have placed their past fought battles around them, using those experiences to create a shield of boundaries.

Talking to the Nine of Wands in Conversation

When the determined Nine of Wands comes forward to speak with you, know that they do so rooted in their personal strength. Their advice will sound like, "Do not give up. Take a moment if you need it, but do not give up," or, "You have clearly been through a lot, so how are you going to use those experiences to motivate you in this moment?" and, "It's okay to protect yourself. Just make sure the walls you built to keep the bad out aren't keeping the good out too."

The Nine of Wands is the perfect persona to speak to when you need reminding of why you are fighting. Bring them forward when you need to be shown how your determination will be rewarded and when it may be best to stand down.

Creating a Personal Connection

Everyone is fighting battles. This we know for sure. But I want you to recall a time when you won the battle completely exhausted.

My moment with the Nine of Wands was when I was working extremely hard to get my health in order. I was seeing doctor after doctor to get them to finally diagnose me with my condition. I was exhausted, but I knew I couldn't stop self-advocating. I knew I had to be strong and persevere. I am now so thankful I did as I finally got the help I needed, but if I had given up, if I had quit, I wouldn't be able to live the wonderful life I do now.

What moment of determination in the face of adversity is coming up for you? When did you have to fight even when you had no fight left in you? That is your Nine of Wands.

Reversal Prompt Questions

How can you release your walls at this moment?

Why are you resistant to seeing how burned out you are?

What is an internal block you have to admitting your frustration?

Ten of Wands

Bearing the weight of burdens, the Ten of Wands carries all of life's responsibilities on their shoulders.

As you can see, the Ten of Wands is a little overwhelmed. The figure holds in their hands ten wands, each representing a responsibility that has been placed upon them. Whether placed there by others or themselves, the figure cannot continue to handle the heaviness of their obligations any longer. Something has got to give; will it be the figure or all they are attempting to carry?

Talking to the Ten of Wands in Conversation

The Ten of Wands is overwhelmed and overworked, so when they step forward, they can't help but give advice rooted in their nature to overcommit. They may say things like, "I can see you are struggling, and I know it is for the people you love, but can you take some pressure off yourself?" or, "Even though you are responsible, it doesn't mean you have to be responsible for everything. How can you prioritize?" and even, "The weight you are carrying is too heavy. Sometimes, you just have to let a few things go in order to move forward."

The Ten of Wands is the perfect persona to talk to when you need to know where in your life you are taking on too much. They can show you where the weight of your responsibilities is straining you and the best options for release.

Creating a Personal Connection

I want you to connect with a time in your life when it felt like everything was on your shoulders. Moments like having to clean the house, do the dishes, take the kids to school, pick the kids up from school, cook the dinner, clean up the dinner, help the kids with homework, put the kids to bed ... wow! All that sounds overwhelming to do on your own, yet there are millions of people doing all that right now, every single day. How exhausting.

That is just one example of a Ten of Wands moment. Another could be being responsible for handling the majority of tasks at work even though you have a team. Or running your own small business and being the social media marketer, the product photographer, the shipping department, and so much more.

The point is you know you are connecting with the Ten of Wands when you feel like you have to be superhuman, even though you know that's impossible but feel you have no other choice.

Reversal Prompt Questions

What is blocking you from sharing the weight you carry with others?

How can you release the mindset that you can't say no?

Why are you resisting freeing yourself from this self-imposed heaviness?

Page of Wands

When you look at every new adventure with enthusiasm and curiosity, you know you are embodying the Page of Wands.

You are meeting the youthful, adventurous, and enthusiastic persona of the wands family, the page. As you can see, they bear a resemblance to the Fool. With a red feather in their cap and a staff of new beginnings in their hands, the page looks toward the future, knowing it holds endless possibilities. Wearing bright yellow clothes of excitement, illumination, and eagerness, the page is eager to explore all that they are passionate about.

Talking to the Page of Wands in Conversation

When this young adventurer joins you for a chat, know that what they lack in experience, they make up for in enthusiasm. They are rooted in their drive to explore any and everything that excites them, so their advice may sound like, "Life is an adventure waiting to be explored. Seek out new experiences," or, "Express yourself with passion and confidence. Share your vision with others, inspiring them with your enthusiasm," and even, "There is nothing wrong with beginnings. You don't have to be an expert. Enjoy the adventure of just starting."

When it comes to needing a motivator to start something new, the Page of Wands is your go-to persona. They will not only help you see where your natural talents lie, but also where you can best use them to eventually inspire others.

Creating a Personal Connection

Like all court cards, you may relate to the Page of Wands as someone you know. Someone with not a lot of experience but a whole lot of passion. If you can't relate to the Page of Wands that way, think about a time in your life when you were genuinely excited for the future. Maybe when you first awakened to spirituality and the idea of all things witchy or mystical sparked your inner child. Or when you just started your small business, and even though you didn't have a lot of experience, every single time you reached a goal, you were filled with excitement.

You will find the Page of Wands in moments of joyful beginnings when following your passions. Can't relate to this? Then use the Page of Wands as your personal messenger to take this opportunity now.

Reversal Prompt Questions

What is blocking your inspiration? How can you tap into your inner spark?

How can you release the mindset that you have to be an expert? How can you step back and enjoy being a student?

Why are you resisting pursuing your passions? What is causing you to stall?

Knight of Wands

Bold and brave, the Knight of Wands traveled the lands searching for his next quest.

The charismatic, eager, and confident persona of the wands family, you can see the passionate energy radiating from him. His bright orange horse rears up to move quickly as the knight faces forward, holding his wand of powerful motivation toward the heavens. He doesn't have time to stop and chat. He is on a quest and must get to his destination quickly while the fires of ambition continue to fuel him.

Talking to the Knight of Wands in Conversation

One thing I learned about the knights early on is they are here for a good time, not a long time. When the Knight of Wands enters the conversation, know that his advice will be rooted in his ambitious and adventurous nature. He may say things like, "It's time to experience something new. Is there room in your life for travel?" or, "Sometimes you just have to be brave and do something exciting," and, "If you keep waiting for the perfect time, you will wait forever. Live your life out loud!"

I know, I know, the Knight of Wand's passion can be a lot to handle, but they are the perfect person to help you see where being a little adventurous in your life could pay off big-time. Use them to fuel your fire and truly live!

Creating a Personal Connection

I won't lie. My personal connection to the Knight of Wands is travel. But that can limit me because he doesn't always show up with that message.

The Knight of Wands can show up in moments when you are feeling confident, curious, brave, and adventurous. These can be moments like being adventurous in your romantic life or being spontaneous and quitting your job to make room for another. In moments where you do something courageous like going skydiving. You get my point. You will know you are connecting with the Knight of Wands when your heart is pounding, you are moving a little fast, and you have to remind yourself to be brave.

If you want to make a connection with the Knight of Wands as a person, I recommend thinking about someone in your life who is charming and romantic but isn't ready to slow down. Someone who is truly fun to be around; they are the life of the party, but they don't see themselves settling anytime soon.

If you have someone in mind, then yeah, that's your Knight of Wands.

Reversal Prompt Questions

Why do you resist being patient? Why are you in such a hurry?

Do you think you have a block when it comes to commitment?

How can you release yourself from allowing your ego to run your life?

Queen of Wands

When creativity meets passion and confidence, you know you have met the Queen of Wands.

You stand in the presence of royalty. The Queen of Wands shines confidently in her yellow gown of cheerfulness while sitting on her throne of abundant and bright sunflowers. Courageous lions are painted behind her as stone carvings sit at her sides. Her wand of power and passion stands tall in her hand, harnessing energy from the heavens. A black cat of all things magic sits in front of her, protecting her from any and all dangers. She is the persona of authenticity, and she rules her kingdom with a warm, open heart.

Talking to the Queen of Wands in Conversation

When this confident queen steps forward to speak with you, open yourself up to her magic, because she is about to spark yours. Rooted in her creative nature, her advice will sound like, "Pick your chin up and step into your power. You are a force to be reckoned with. Don't let them make you doubt yourself," or, "You can create the life you want, but it must start in your heart center. Take a moment, see the life you want, now take real steps to create it," and, "You radiate magic. Harness it and let other people see you. Go out in the world and find your fellow magicians."

Creating a Personal Connection

When it comes to connecting the Queen of Wands to someone you may know in real life, think of a person who is cheerful and charismatic and radiates confidence. Someone you just gravitate to because their authenticity is addicting.

When I think of the Queen of Wands, I think of my friend Taylor. She is a powerful loving force of nature, and I can't help but aspire to have even a slice of her confidence one day. She is brave and unapologetically herself. She is a kind and fair businesswoman who treats all her employees with respect. She is someone I am proud to call a friend, and weirdly enough, I know she would say the same about me.

Do you have someone in your life who has those same characteristics? If not, I encourage you to form a connection by thinking about moments in your life that were filled with passion, creativity, confidence, and maybe even sensuality.

Moments like leading your team at work in finding a creative solution to a problem or going out with your friends to a paint-and-sip event. You can even find the queen in moments when you put on some lingerie and stepped into your power as a sexual being. She's there all right. And lastly, if you are a practitioner of magic like me, you can connect with the Queen of Wands every time you step into your inner power and begin a ritual working.

Reversal Prompt Questions

How can you release your feelings of insecurity?

What is blocking you from harnessing your personal power?

Why are you resistant to believing in magic? Even if it is your own?

King of Wands

"Give yourself permission to lead a life of courage and self-confidence," proclaims the King of Wands.

As you look upon the ruler of wands, you will see that he does not face you. He chooses to look outward toward all he has created through experience. His wand of stability and power is grounded in the earth below him as a salamander sits calmly by his side, representing his never-wavering resilience. He is a passionate king, as you can see by his fiery clothes, but through experience, he has become the master of his creative flame and uses it to inspire those around him.

He is the embodiment of all fairy-tale kings with his ability to lead and motivate those around him to live a life inspired.

Talking to the King of Wands in Conversation

When this charismatic king comes forward to advise you, know that the advice will be inspirational. The King of Wands is rooted in his ability to master his creative passion and focus it in a positive direction. Because of this, his advice will sound like, "How can you channel your passion and create something that will inspire others?" or, "There is a leader in you. How can you use your experience to show others the way?" and even, "Is there a mentor you can seek right now to help you with this?"

The King of Wands may be a powerful ally to bring forward when you need someone in your corner. When you need someone to remind you of how powerful you are and all that you are capable of creating. Sometimes, we just need someone to help us direct our efforts in the right direction.

Creating a Personal Connection

If you want to think of someone in your life who would resemble the King of Wands, think about someone who is charismatic, funny, confident, attractive, and lives a life others aspire to have. If you have someone in your life who resembles even a few of these characteristics, you have your King of Wands.

I personally like to connect with the energies of the King of Wands when I need to embody confidence, inspiration, and authority. Moments like when I am being a spiritual coach for my clients or facilitating a Reiki class. Moments when I am directing a photo shoot for my brand or helping others build their own.

These are the moments when I find the King of Wands shows up in my life. What is a moment in your life when you felt like a real leader and, in doing so, inspired others to be the same?

Reversal Prompt Questions

How can you release your feelings of arrogance and superiority?

Why are you resistant to letting others lead? Why do you have to have control?

How can you overcome your internal block of self-doubt? What is the root of this insecurity?

Chapter Five
The Suit of Swords

The suit of the mind and all the complexities it contains.

This air suit is one that, unfortunately, a lot of people dread to see in a reading. As a Libra sun, I think this suit gets a bad rep, but I understand that not everyone needs to be reminded of what's on their mind.

Dealing with themes of painful memories, inner mindsets, and facts over feelings, this suit forces you to speak your thoughts out loud.

Asking you to cut through the illusions of life and reveal your truth, the swords bring all challenges and mental conflicts to the light. With personas of clear thinking, logical decision-making, and honest communication, the swords encourage you to face your thoughts and trust in the power of your mind.

Ace of Swords

The persona of a new healthy mindset, we embrace this breakthrough of clarity and call it the Ace of Swords.

The Ace of Swords, just like all the other aces, does speak of new beginnings as divine gifts, but this time, it starts within the mind and radiates outward. As you can see, the hand of the divine holds the sword of powerful truth upright as a crown of authority and confidence sits atop it. With olive branches of peace and palm branches of victory sitting securely on the crown, you see that this gift of a new understanding will bring nothing but success. The background is a neutral grey, as small mountains of future challenges are the only landscape to be seen.

The Ace of Swords is a mighty persona of newfound personal truth, clear communication, and fresh mindsets.

Talking to the Ace of Swords in Conversation

When the gift of mental clarity comes forward, you know you are about to talk with the embodiment of personal empowerment. They are rooted in their authority of all things logical and clearly communicated, so this is where their advice will stem from. They will ask you questions such as, "What is your inner truth when it comes to this situation?" or, "How can you reclaim your power?" and, "Now that you have this new mindset, how are you going to tackle problems directly and find solutions?"

The Ace of Swords is the bringer of mental clarity, so call on them when you need to see things from a new perspective. They can help you find confidence in your truth and show you how that truth can shape your reality.

Creating a Personal Connection

Can you remember a time when a new mindset suddenly helped you see your life or situation differently? Or when you finally decided to own your truth, and it gave you unbeatable confidence? If yes, then you have been in the presence of the Ace of Swords.

The Ace of Swords finds us in everyday moments when we reconnect to our divine truth. When we realize, "Hey, I don't have to think this way," or, "Who said it has to be this way? I can do it differently." Moments such as reframing trauma that allows you to be empowered rather than paralyzed. Or standing up to people who belittle you and deciding you won't be spoken to that way. Even moments when you step into a leadership role and become confident in your communication skills.

These are all moments where the Ace of Swords can be seen. Moments of truth, authority, honesty, and mental clarity.

Reversal Prompt Questions

What is a mental block that you are currently facing keeping you in self-doubt?

How can you release this negative mindset?

Why are you resistant to communicating your thoughts and ideas to those around you?

Two of Swords

In moments of complete stillness and isolation, you will meet the Two of Swords.

As you can see, the Two of Swords is in a place of in-between. They sit here on a stone seat with no life around them except the vast waters of their emotions that flow behind them. They use their hands to cross over their heart, blocking it, and yield a sword in each hand as if to warn any who dare get near. Blindfolded by choice, they sit in darkness. To block out anything and everything to avoid making any sort of hasty decision. They seem peaceful here because of the blue shade of the night sky. You are meeting them here, in this moment of conscious pause. They needed this moment of stillness for them to go into their subconscious and see their true image.

They entered this moment being unclear of what they wanted, but when they are ready, they will lay down their swords and remove the blindfold, awakening to their truth.

Talking to the Two of Swords in Conversation

The personification of liminal space has arrived, and they want to have a little chat. When the Two of Swords comes forward, they do so rooted in the in-between. They are inaction personified, so their advice will stem from this. They will come forward and say things like, "Just take a moment to connect with your inner truth; no need to rush this," or, "What are you avoiding? What don't you want to see?" and, "Sometimes deciding not to make a choice is a choice in itself."

The Two of Swords can be a good friend to lean on when you find yourself in a place of in-between. They can show you where pausing may benefit you and where it can harm you. Call on them when you need a moment to center yourself and speak with your inner truth before moving forward.

Creating a Personal Connection

We all have moments when we just need a second to find out what we really want.

These moments can look like weighing your options before accepting a job offer or taking a moment to see how you really feel before ending a relationship.

The Two of Swords can also look like moments of avoidance or uncertainty. Such as not wanting to say yes to a marriage proposal because you aren't 100 percent sure they are your person. Or avoiding naming your business because you can't find one that resonates on a soul level.

These moments don't always have to be so extreme, either. They can be taking a step back when you want to rebrand your social media accounts or are being indecisive on whether or not to cut your hair.

Little or big, the moments when you just need a second to figure out how you really feel, those are when you meet the Two of Swords.

Reversal Prompt Questions

Are you ready to remove the block keeping you from making a decision?

How can you remove the resistance you feel when it comes to seeking closure?

What actions do you need to take to face the problems you are hiding from right now?

Three of Swords

The persona of piercing heartache, loss, and sorrow, the Three of Swords remains large and open still.

I say large because there is no denying the size of the red heart in front of you. Behind it, you see rain clouds pouring, implying that the pain is still very present and emotionally torturous, but there is no lightning, no hail, no environmental damage. Has the brunt of the storm passed? Three swords pierce the heart, representing the impact and strength of the pain felt not only within the body but the mind as well.

It is important to note that the swords do not take up the entirety of the heart nor is the heart closed off from being able to accept more. There is still room for love, but will the Three of Swords take that risk?

Talking to the Three of Swords in Conversation

No one wants to speak to heartbreak, but if they come forward, it's best to at least acknowledge their presence. The Three of Swords is past heartbreak personified. They know a thing or two about suffering, so when they give advice, it's from a place of been there, done that. They will say things like, "The pain you feel is real; it hurts, but it doesn't have to hurt forever," or, "Your capacity to love is larger than what this pain is telling you," and, "The pain you have been avoiding feeling is here now; see it, feel it, release it."

When the Three of Swords wants to speak with you, they do so because they see the pain you hold inside and do not want it to stunt your growth. They know you are capable of immeasurable love, so use them to help you see the pain and then release it.

Creating a Personal Connection

I feel silly asking you to make a personal connection to heartbreak, but hey, that's what this section is for, right? Think about the pain you feel not only inside your body but inside your mind as well. Pain that was so intense it may have caused you to disconnect from your body entirely and live inside that safe haven that is your brain. Acknowledge it. Connect with it and know when you do, you are making a lifetime connection with the Three of Swords.

Reversal Prompt Questions

What is blocking you from allowing yourself to heal from these wounds of the past?

How can you release the mindset that is keeping you from confronting your heartbreak?

Why are you resistant to forgiving those who have hurt you? How can you work through this?

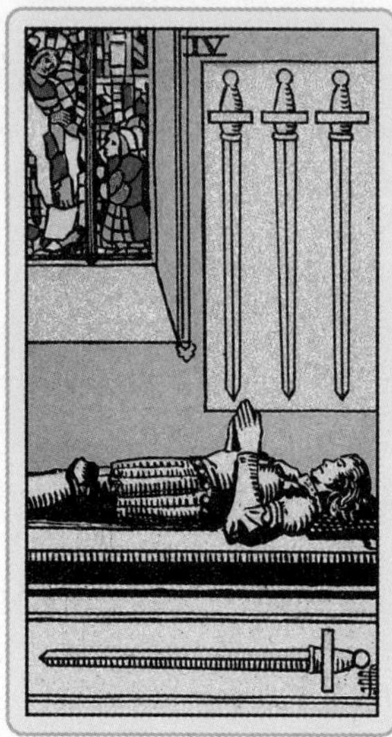

Four of Swords

When rest meets retreat, you know you have met the Four of Swords.

You are meeting the Four of Swords right as they partake in a hard-earned break. They have been through it, as you can see from the swords hanging above them. It's time to take a step inward and take a restful breather. They do not rest in a forest or at the bottom of an ocean, no—they rest in a sacred space, as you can see by the church window. They came here for healing. They are going within themselves to reset and recuperate from all they have been through.

Sounds great! Sign me up!

Talking to the Four of Swords in Conversation

When the Four of Swords enters the conversation, they do so from their place of rest. Their advice will always focus on finding a safe place to just pause. You will receive advice such as, "I think now would be a great time to go off and meditate on this," or, "You have been dealing with a lot; take a step back for a while and recenter," and, "It doesn't have to happen today; take some time and recover."

It doesn't matter what you bring to the Four of Swords; they will always be team to take a break.

Creating a Personal Connection

I know you may not relate, but I am just going to say it. A great personal connection you can make with the Four of Swords is meditating.

It doesn't have to be a "sitting in silence" type of meditation, even though that would be a perfect experience. It could be meditating while on a walk or meditating while in your room listening to the latest binaural beats YouTube video. The key here is being alone, grounding your energy, and allowing yourself to rest without feeling guilty.

When was the last time you gave yourself a moment like this?

Reversal Prompt Questions

Why are you resistant to real rest? What emotions come up for you when you think of taking a break?

How can you remove the block that the only time you have value is when you are of service?

How can you release the mindset that you have to put others' needs above your own?

Five of Swords

The persona of winning at all costs, the Five of Swords stands tall, but was all this conflict worth it?

As you can see, there are several figures present at this moment. We have a clear victor holding more swords than he can carry, as well as two other figures who face away in despair as they abandon their weapons. The clouds are sharp and grey as the water greets the light blue sky. This moment feels sad even though someone has clearly gained the upper hand—but at what cost?

Talking to the Five of Swords in Conversation

When the Five of Swords steps forward, you are speaking with the two sides of a battle personified, so their advice will be rooted in this. It will say things like, "Is it better to walk away from the situation or stand your ground?" or, "I know you feel like you have lost, but was it truly worth winning in the first place?" and, "You had to stand up for yourself, even if they got hurt. At least you didn't, right?"

The Five of Swords may be difficult to speak with because you are speaking with both the winner and the loser in the situation, but here is the thing: you are really speaking to your mental perception of the events that have transpired.

Creating a Personal Connection

Moments of defeat are easily recalled. They were painful, so we tend to remember them in hopes of avoiding future pain. I say this because when you are connecting to the Five of Swords, I want you to connect to the loss side, of course, but also the winning side.

What is a moment in your life when you did indeed win, but it was at the cost of another? Was it when you got the promotion over someone else, not because you necessarily earned it but because you were blessed with charisma? Or when you won the war of words with your partner but ended up maybe causing more damage than you intended?

These are moments when you will find connection with the Five or Swords. Where there is a battle, you can win or lose, but is it worth fighting in the first place?

Reversal Prompt Questions

How can you remove the block keeping you in this place of resentment?

Why are you resistant to compromising?

How can you release yourself from this conflict?

Six of Swords

Moving on from turmoil toward tranquility, the Six of Swords sees hope on the horizon.

You are meeting the Six of Swords right as they embark on a journey of healing. The memories of what they have been through are clearly still on the boat with them when looking at the six swords present, but they are moving forward anyway. The boat moves away from the rocky waters beside it to the steady waters ahead. The figures in the boat face away and cover themselves; they aren't looking back, only forward and inward. They know they are leaving a difficult situation and are ready to go somewhere safer, even if their baggage is coming with them.

Talking to the Six of Swords in Conversation

When the Six of Swords comes forward for a chat, you know a transition is on the way. They can't help it, it's who they are. They will give advice such as, "It's time to move on; you don't have to forget, but you do have to move," or, "Things are really emotionally overwhelming; can you go to a safe place?" and, "Change is always going to be scary, but it's time. You have to do this for you."

The Six of Swords is the perfect persona to speak with when you know it's time to move on but are scared to do so. They can help you navigate the situation logically and find a safe option for you. When you need help finding a new direction, call forward the Six of Swords to navigate the waters with you.

Creating a Personal Connection

Sometimes you don't know where you are going, you just have to go. These are the moments where you will find the Six of Swords. Leaving difficult situations can be hard, but you need to do it anyway. Yes, it can be uncomfortable and even emotional, but you must be brave and start the journey anyway.

You will find the Six of Swords in moments like leaving a painful relationship, moving out of a toxic household, finding shelter with friends, and even unfollowing social media accounts that bring you mental stress.

The Six of Swords is in everyday moments when you transition from a place of pain to a place of relief. When was a time you found yourself making this transition?

Reversal Prompt Questions

What is blocking you from healing your emotional baggage?

Why do you have resistance to leaving this painful situation? Why are you stuck here?

How can you release yourself from these fears and anxieties that are holding you back?

Seven of Swords

Navigating the world with strategy and deception, the Seven of Swords is the persona of stealth.

Someone so cunning must be dishonest, right? Well, that is the popular opinion when it comes to the Seven of Swords. For some reason, they have a really bad reputation for dishonesty, deception, and sneaky selfishness. I mean, I can understand this if you are seeing them under the right circumstances, but for general purposes, they are just a really good strategist. I say this because you are meeting them right when they are carefully sneaking away with the enemy's weapons. The background is not black, which would suggest that this is happening at night; no, the Seven of Swords is so stealthy they are able to do this in broad daylight. Do they personally need five swords? No. They are clearly trying to gain the upper hand here, and even though we don't really know their motives for this, we can still see that they are very resourceful and motivated.

These are not bad qualities to have when facing obstacles.

Talking to the Seven of Swords in Conversation

When the cunning thief comes forward, it's best to at least hear them out; I mean, clearly, they have learned a thing or two. The Seven of Swords is rooted in their ability to be secretive, so they may provide advice such as, "Sometimes it's just better to avoid conflict," or, "You can't get in trouble if you don't get caught," and, "Find a way to be flexible in this situation. Think ahead and pay close attention to those around you."

You may not want to speak with them, but the Seven of Swords is a great person to call upon when you need to be a little strategic in your life to gain the upper hand or when you want to see where there may be deception and how you can uncover it. Just make sure you are prepared for the answer.

Creating a Personal Connection

During our lives, we have all had to be a little sneaky or hide our true feelings. This is just part of the human experience. I am not saying it's good, and I am not saying it's bad. I am just saying I feel like we can all relate to this experience.

When I was trying to leave a previous position, I will be honest: I hid my feelings and made plans with a future employer. I mean, my boss clearly knew what was going on, but in my head, I was being so deceptive and sneaky. At the end of the day, when I was ready, I let them know I needed to move on. Sure, they were disappointed, but they already knew it was going to happen. I sometimes think about what would have happened if I had just been honest about my feelings instead of feeling like I had to hide. Clearly, things worked out exactly how they were meant to, so why did I feel the need to be sneaky?

When was a moment in your life when you felt you had to be the same? Where have you aligned with the Seven of Swords?

Reversal Prompt Questions

How can you release yourself from the lies and embrace the truth of the situation?

What is blocking you from taking responsibility?

Why are you resistant to letting out all the secrets?

Eight of Swords

Bound by fear and doubt, the Eight of Swords is the persona of self-created limitations.

You are meeting the Eight of Swords as they stand in a mental prison of their own making. As you can see, the swords are not in front of them, keeping them trapped—no, they are beside them. This is a self-imposed restriction. They wear a red dress, so you know they are powerful, yet they have bound themselves with a white cloth and covered their eyes, restraining themselves from who they really are as well as their emotions. They have removed themselves from their home, as you can see it lie grey in the background.

Why have they put themselves here, and why will they not remove the blindfold and ties that bind them? Why are they staying here?

Talking to the Eight of Swords in Conversation

When the Eight of Swords comes forward, you are speaking with the embodiment of self-sabotaging mental patterns. This is who they are, and because of this, they are great at showing you where you are holding yourself back. They will say things like, "I know you feel trapped right now. What can you do to release yourself?" or, "Things feel hopeless, and you don't want to really see what's going on, but this is harming you," and, "Your perspective isn't always going to reflect the reality of the situation. Can you try to look at this differently?"

The Eight of Swords knows a thing or two about being imprisoned, even if it is just in your mind. Connect with them when you need to see where your self-sabotaging patterns are manifesting and how you can release yourself.

Creating a Personal Connection

You will find yourself connecting with the Eight of Swords in the moments when you really are trapped. Trapped in a thought process, trapped in a situation, and trapped in a relationship.

You have control over all these things, but your mind tells you that you don't. Moments such as feeling like you can't leave a job because you don't have another lined up or that you can't cancel on a friend you promised you'd meet up with even though you aren't feeling well. Even moments when you can't see the bright side of things because lately it's just been one bad thing after another. All these moments share the energies of being stuck and having no control, even though you do.

The Eight of Swords is the persona of illusion. Where have you seen them show up in your life?

Reversal Prompt Questions

What is blocking you from freeing yourself?

Why are you so resistant to moving forward, even if it's painful?

How can you release the mindset that is keeping you imprisoned?

Nine of Swords

Oh, anxiety, my haunting nighttime friend, I see you have come to visit again.

Better known as the persona of anxiety, fear, and negative mindsets, the Nine of Swords is having a difficult time. You are meeting them in their bedroom as they have just awoken from a nightmare, or did they even get to sleep? The nine swords above their head show you just how painful their mindset is. The background is black, representing how dark their thoughts really are. But they do not lie in a bed filled with nails or thorns; no, they lie on a stable frame and a soft mattress, covered in a warm blanket of roses. See, their thoughts are not reflecting their reality.

Their mind is tricking them, and only they have the power to change this.

Talking to the Nine of Swords in Conversation

Try not to fear when the Nine of Swords comes forward to speak to you; they do so in hopes of helping you see just how powerless these fears really are. Because of this, their advice may sound like, "Are your thoughts reflecting the reality of the situation?" or, "I know you can't help but think about this, but can you find someone to help you?" and, "Remember it's facts over feelings—or in this case, thoughts. What are the facts?"

We all have fears that can keep us up at night. Talk to the Nine of Swords when you need to face these fears head-on and remove their power.

Creating a Personal Connection

As someone with anxiety, it feels weird to ask you to make a personal connection, but I truly want you to form a relationship with this persona.

When can you recall experiencing feelings of worry, fear, and maybe even guilt or shame? Was it when you were so worried about a parent or sibling that you couldn't sleep until you'd heard from them? Or maybe when you studied so hard for a test and found yourself anxiously awaiting the results.

I find that the Nine of Swords loves to make an appearance in my life when I am more worried about how others perceive me than how I perceive myself. Like when I worried no one would like this book or that it would never even be published because who really cares what I have to say? These were the thoughts that kept me up at night and tried to create my reality. I clearly didn't let them win, and you shouldn't let yours win either.

What are the thoughts keeping you up at night? What are some moments when you looked anxiety right in the face? Are they coming to mind? Good! Then you have indeed met the Nine of Swords.

Reversal Prompt Questions

What is blocking you from overcoming your trauma?

How can you release this negative mindset keeping you in fear?

Why are you resisting reaching out for help?

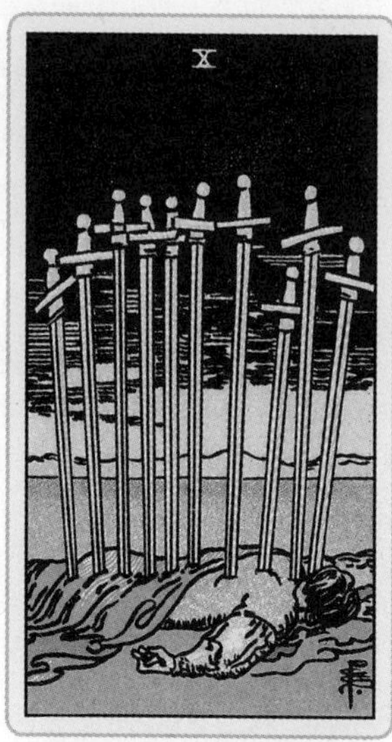

Ten of Swords

Lying in their suffering, the Ten of Swords is the persona of painful closures that lead to eventual renewals.

You are looking at a cruel and gruesome scene. You are meeting the Ten of Swords at the lowest point in their life. As you can see, they are suffering. They have been hurt not once, not three times, but ten times. This is more than any one person can bear, and we see the figure has succumbed to their injuries. They are not fighting or attempting to stand; no, they are lying there in defeat.

Looking at the background, you may find a small glimmer of hope as a dark black sky begins to turn yellow, peaking across the horizon. The water is still, telling us that the last blow didn't just happen but that the effects of it can clearly still be felt.

This is a moment of recurring pain, and such patterns do not disappear overnight. The mental effects will take time to heal, but healing is always possible.

Talking to the Ten of Swords in Conversation

I won't lie; the Ten of Swords isn't the most positive or uplifting persona to speak with, but what they lack in joy, they make up for in awareness of internal suffering. When they speak to you, it may sound like, "Look at your pain right in the eyes. Acknowledge all that you have been through," or, "There is no ignoring that you are hurt, now what are you going to do with this pain?" and, "You are carrying all these painful moments with you, they linger inside of you. How can you release them?"

The Ten of Swords is your partner in pain. They see yours as clearly as you can see theirs. Call on them when you need to look at the painful parts of your life. When you need to heal, what cannot be seen but felt? They will be your companion in the dark and help you awaken to the light.

Creating a Personal Connection

When it comes to connecting to the Ten of Swords, I don't want you to just connect to a painful moment but rather one that felt like a final blow. When you couldn't imagine taking on anymore, and then *boom,* the universe added another sword into your back. This is where you will connect with the Ten of Swords. This is how you will forever remember the energy of this card. Sorry in advance.

Reversal Prompt Questions

What past pains are you struggling to release and move on from?

What is blocking you from changing your mindset and focusing on hope rather than despair?

How can you remove the resistance you feel to saying goodbye to those who are causing you pain? How can you reach out to support systems for help?

Page of Swords

With a curious mind and an independent soul, the Page of Swords stands alone.

Young, bright, and witty, the Page of Swords stands alone on their hill of higher thinking. The quick winds of clever communication flow through their hair. They hold their sword of sharp intellect toward their chest as if protecting their youthful heart. Standing in front of a blue sky filled with clouds of fresh ideas, the page's feet are grounded into the earth below them, letting everyone know they are grounded in their ways. They wear clothes of red and yellow, making sure everyone can see how confident and energetic they are. The Page of Swords does not need anyone to stand beside them as they are a freethinker, and sometimes that means standing apart from the crowd.

As a quick thinker and clear communicator, there is nothing this persona can't achieve once they put their mind to it.

Talking to the Page of Swords in Conversation

Rooted in their nature to bring new perspectives, the Page of Swords comes forward to give advice such as, "What new subject of learning is calling to you right now?" or, "How could being honest and direct with someone benefit this situation," and even, "Stand your ground on your truths. Not everyone is going to think the way you do, and that's okay."

Call forth this sometimes blunt persona when you need to find your curiosity for life again. Not only will they point you in the right direction, they will also show you where your mental energy is best spent.

Creating a Personal Connection

I think we can all relate to the Page of Swords when it comes to standing our ground on our beliefs, even if those beliefs are fairly new to us. Still, there is just something about working toward a new mindset and then having to put in the work to defend that mindset from others or even old ways of thinking. If you can't relate to the Page of Swords in that way, just think about a time in your life when you had to be a quick learner and a slow conscientious talker. When you were able to pick up a skill quickly, but also made sure you didn't get a big ego.

Sometimes, because of the page's youth, they can be a little bit defensive, so if you're struggling to make a connection with their other aspects, just think of a time when you had your own walls up, even if you weren't under attack per se. If you want to connect to the Page of Swords by thinking of a person in your life, just think of someone who is very intelligent and may be starting a new subject of study. Someone with a natural curiosity for life who communicates clearly. You don't have to ask them what's on their mind, they will happily share with you.

If someone comes to mind, wonderful! You are forming a personal connection with the Page of Swords.

Reversal Prompt Questions

What is blocking you from speaking your truth?

Why are you resisting healing the inner wounds that cause you to be so defensive?

How can you release the mindset that others will only like you if you take on their personalities?

Knight of Swords

Riding with relentless determination, the Knight of Swords charges forward.

As you can see, someone needs to tell the Knight of Swords there is no fire, and they can calm down. You are meeting the knight right as they are racing toward their next quest. The wind behind them blows not only the trees but also the clouds above, showing you just how quickly the knight's mind is racing at this very moment. Their horse rushes forward as the knight raises their sword of powerful intellect toward the heavens, allowing the clarity of their mission to be divinely guided. The Knight of Swords is determined and doesn't allow the mountain of challenges to break his focus.

The persona of swift decisions, the Knight of Swords is known to think quickly and act even quicker.

Talking to the Knight of Swords in Conversation

If the Knight of Swords slows down to have a quick chat, know that their advice will be rooted in their boldness and need for sudden change. This means they will bring messages like, "It's time to take action; don't overthink it, just do it," or, "How would your truth move this situation forward? What would it change?" and even, "Sometimes you have to block everything and everyone out in order to gain momentum. Now is the time to do this."

The embodiment of quick movement and focused determination, the Knight of Swords is the perfect companion when you need things to move fast but in a beneficial direction. They can show you where to go and the quickest path to get you there.

Creating a Personal Connection

Sometimes you need to move fast, and then sometimes you need to move faster than fast, if that makes sense. When connecting with the Knight of Swords, I want you to think of a time in your life when you felt you had to rush, and if you didn't rush, what you were working toward simply wouldn't happen. Like a time when you had to rush to the airport or you would miss your flight, or when you had to race the clock to turn in a paper on time. These are all moments when you can find the Knight of Swords as well as in moments of intense focus and bold action. This can feel like turning off all distractions to complete a task or deciding to speak your truth to someone you had been avoiding.

When connecting with the Knight of Swords as a person in your life, think about someone who speaks their mind, makes decisions quickly, and isn't afraid to try out new things. Someone like that newly matched date who took you go-cart racing or your friend who knows everything about changing social media trends.

Who is coming to mind? What past experiences have you found yourself embodying the Knight of Swords in?

Reversal Prompt Questions

How can you remove the block that keeps you from being present in the moment?

Why are you resisting slowing down and taking control of your thoughts?

How can you release yourself from being so combative with others?

Queen of Swords

When one is honest, open, and wise, they can call themselves the Queen of Swords.

You stand here in front of the queen, who wears a golden butterfly crown of transformation cloaked in clouds of clear ideas and sits on a throne of divine connection. She holds one hand out as if welcoming you closer, but don't get too close; in her other hand, she holds a sword of protective boundaries and strict principles. She has no problem using her absolute truth to either raise someone up or strike them down.

The persona of integrity and clarity, the Queen of Swords has used her past pains to build herself up and inspire those around her to do the same.

Talking to the Queen of Swords in Conversation

It's time to get to the truth of the matter, says the Queen of Swords. The queen is rooted in her loving truth, so she will bring messages such as, "Speak your mind, but do it with kindness. People appreciate honesty, and it will help you avoid misunderstandings," or, "Step into your power and trust in your own strength and abilities—you can handle more than you think," and even, "Your past pain gave you the gifts of perspective and discernment. Try to see things as they really are. Even if it's tough, honesty will guide you in the right direction."

She may not be your favorite queen, but she is one who will get to the truth. Talk to her when you seek to think logically about a situation. She will help cut through the clouds and see what's really going on.

Creating a Personal Connection

When connecting to the Queen of Swords, you may find yourself thinking of someone who is blunt, and a little opinionated. I am not saying the Queen of Swords isn't these things, so it's fine to connect to her in this way, but she is also independent, confident, and someone who stands up for what's right.

If you can't connect with the queen as a person, connect with her in moments of your life when you had to set a personal boundary, use your pain to empathize with another's perspective, and even be a little brutally honest with someone.

As a Libra sun, I can't tell you how many people connect me with the Queen of Swords. At first, I was resistant to this because, as an intuitive, I love the Queen of Cups, and as a witch, I am drawn to the magic of the Queen of Wands. But after sitting with my own truth, I was able to see the resemblance. One, I love a good personal boundary. Two, I use my past painful experiences to open up to people and show them that they are not alone. And three, I am always up for a debate, especially if that debate revolves around a clear injustice. So yeah, I guess I can see the connection.

What is your connection? Where can you see yourself in the Queen of Swords, or where has she shown up in your life?

Reversal Prompt Questions

What is blocking you from using your truth to build others up? Not tear them down?

Why are you resistant to seeing things from others' perspectives?

How can you release yourself from illusions or false beliefs?

King of Swords

To be fair, honest, and analytical is to be the King of Swords.

Sitting before you is the king of the mind. He is disciplined in his thoughts; as you can see, there is so wind blowing in the background. All is calm, stable, and grounded. The king does not place his feet on a stone throne but on the ground beneath him; he will not be swayed. His golden crown of authority rests atop a red veil of confidence and leadership. The king holds up his sword of honest communication and powerful logic as he is the king who rules his kingdom with integrity and authenticity.

The embodiment of responsibility and maturity, you will find the King of Swords in moments of everyday life that require you to be both.

Talking to the King of Swords in Conversation

When the king of knowing everything enters the conversation, it's a good bet he is here to remind you to think clearly. The King of Swords is rooted in his mastery of the mind, so he will give advice such as, "What are the facts of the situation? Take a moment to think things through before deciding. Clear thinking will guide you to the best choices," or, "How are your feelings clouding your judgement? Try to keep a cool head and stay rational," and, "Even if it's tough, try to be fair and balanced when making big decisions."

Again, the King of Swords may not be your favorite, but he is one who will bring logic into a situation that may be fueled by emotion. Seek him out when you need to not only see the truth of the situation but find a fair resolution for all.

Creating a Personal Connection

When making a connection with the King of Swords, think: facts. There may be a person in your life who, yes, isn't very emotionally available, but they always have the facts. That is your King of Swords.

If you don't have a King of Swords in your life to create a connection with, think about a time when you had to say to yourself, "Facts over feelings." My therapist *loves* to remind me of this mindset, and even though I know it helps, I still get a little annoyed. But it is the perfect connection to make with the King of Swords. What is an experience when you had to take a deep breath and remember the truth of the situation, even if your emotions were telling you something different?

This is your King of Swords connection. A moment of clear thinking and responsible action.

Reversal Prompt Questions

How can you release your need for control?

What is blocking you from releasing your quick judgements of others?

Why are you resisting taking accountability for your own actions?

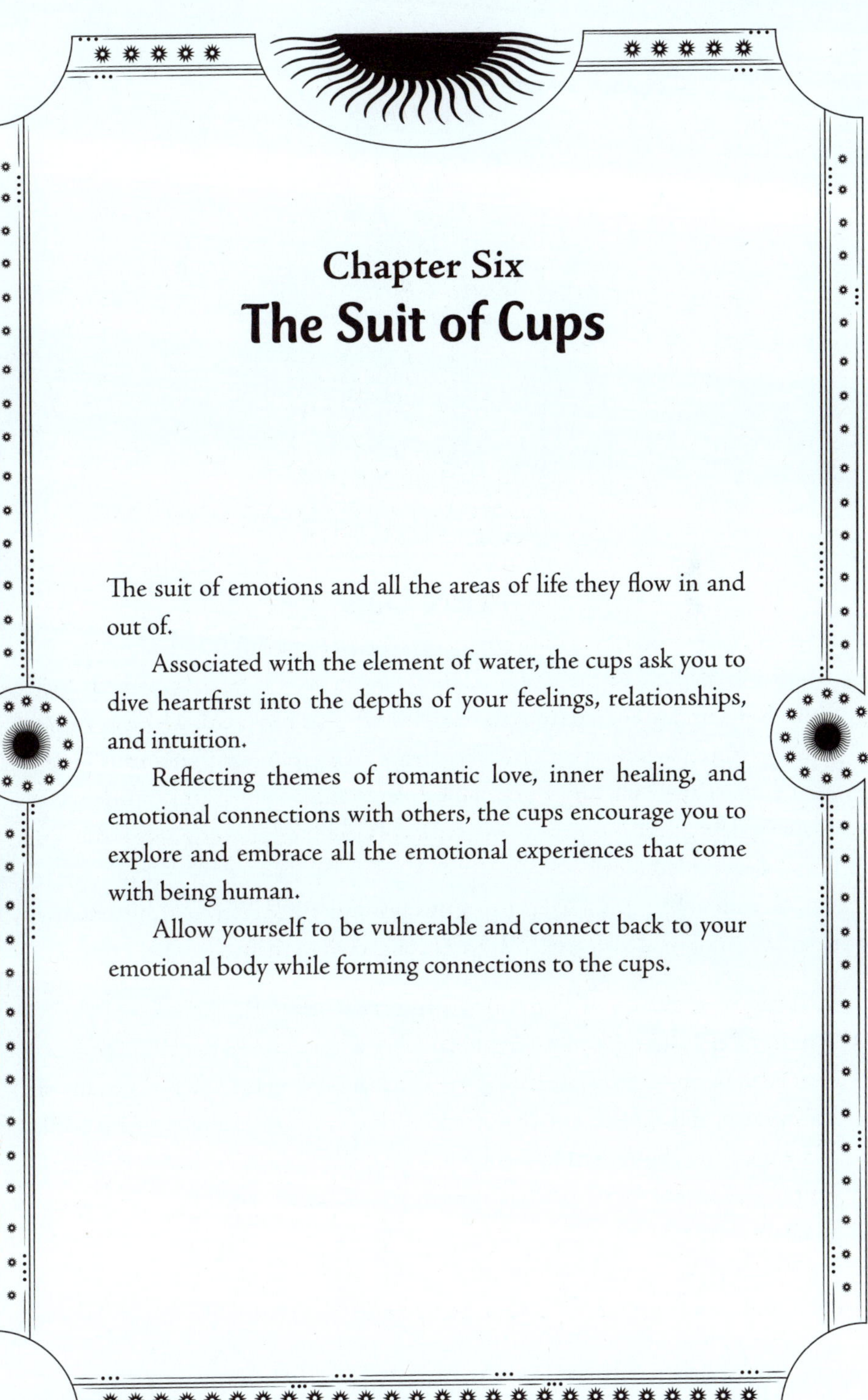

Chapter Six

The Suit of Cups

The suit of emotions and all the areas of life they flow in and out of.

Associated with the element of water, the cups ask you to dive heartfirst into the depths of your feelings, relationships, and intuition.

Reflecting themes of romantic love, inner healing, and emotional connections with others, the cups encourage you to explore and embrace all the emotional experiences that come with being human.

Allow yourself to be vulnerable and connect back to your emotional body while forming connections to the cups.

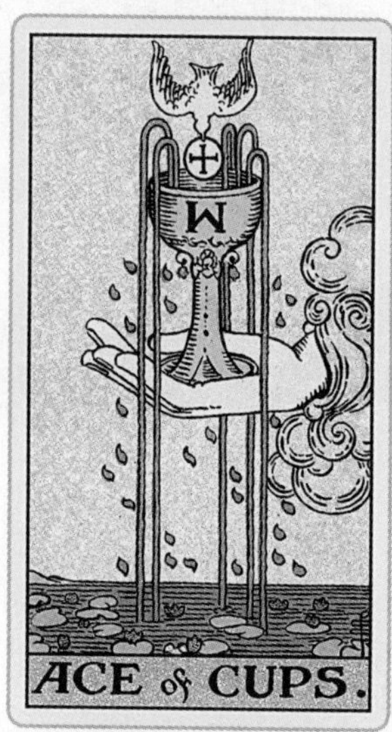

Ace of Cups

Meet the personification of awakened love, the Ace of Cups.

Just by looking at the Ace of Cups, you can see its connection with Spirit, from the hand descending from the clouds to the pure white dove diving into the ornate chalice itself. Can you feel the overflow of emotional fulfillment pouring out of the sides of this holy grail lookalike? As the waters of compassion flow downward, you can see the representation of new life connecting with the water lilies blooming below.

As with all the aces, the Ace of Cups brings a fresh start, but this one stems from our emotional selves and all that is connected to them.

Talking to the Ace of Cups in Conversation

When the persona of a new emotional opportunity enters the chat, it's best to greet them with open arms. The Ace of Cups always brings news of a fresh start, and because of this, their advice will sound like, "Is your heart open so that others may enter?" or, "Embrace your feelings, no matter how intense they may seem. Let your emotions wash over you," and even, "You are surrounded by divine love and guidance. Trust in Spirit."

Find the Ace of Cups when you are ready to open your heart to the relationships and new beginnings the universe is lining up for you. They can show you where emotional fulfillment can be found and even where it already resides in your present life.

Creating a Personal Connection

I won't even try to hide the love I have for the Ace of Cups. Every time I connect with it in real life, it is a beautiful, loving moment.

One of my favorite moments of connection was when I was in Costa Rica on a spiritual retreat and participated in a somatic breath work workshop. It was a profound experience of divine connection, emotional release, and soul renewal. This moment allowed me to open my heart not only to the universe but also to those around me. I created lifelong bonds with the people I met on that retreat, and I know wholeheartedly the entire trip was a gift from Spirit.

Now, you may be rolling your eyes and thinking, "Not everyone can go to Costa Rica, Sam," and believe me, I get it. That was a once-in-a-lifetime opportunity for me, but spiritual retreats are not the only moments when you can meet the Ace of Cups. They can be found in everyday moments like creating new friendships, starting up romantic relationships, and even in moments of healing, such as inner child work.

The point is that you will meet the Ace of Cups in moments of emotional beginnings. This doesn't mean they have to be life-changing moments, just moments when you feel something, maybe even on a soul level.

Reversal Prompt Questions

How can you work through the block you have when it comes to opening your heart?

Why are you resistant to being emotionally vulnerable?

How can you release the mindset that you have to overgive emotionally and underreceive?

Two of Cups

The embodiment of mutual affection, the Two of Cups personifies connection and partnership.

You are meeting the Two of Cups right when the two figures are beginning their union. The sky is light blue with peace and clarity as it meets a green fertile landscape. The two figures stand in the middle of the hill, representing how balanced and stable their relationship is, while a red-winged lion's head sits above them, symbolizing not only the courage the two must have to begin this union but that the union itself is divinely guided. Wreaths of victorious love adorn the figures' heads as they bring their chalices of shared feelings together, creating an emotional bond.

They are connecting in this moment. Coming together in respect and affection, the two are equal partnership manifested.

Talking to the Two of Cups in Conversation

The Two of Cups is always a welcomed persona in conversation because they bring advice rooted in a successful union. They will give advice such as, "The most successful partnerships are the ones with mutual respect," or, "It takes both people being equally emotionally invested and open to make a union work," and, "What are you contributing to the personal relationships in your life?"

Connect with the Two of Cups when you need to see where a partnership would be mutually beneficial. They not only show you where but also how to maintain one that is emotionally healthy.

Creating a Personal Connection

Did anyone else hear, "When two becomes one," or was it just me?

Well, even if it was just me, it is in those moments when you will connect with the Two of Cups, when two individuals show up and agree to join forces. This can look like a romantic relationship, sure, but it can also be a business partnership, a friendship, or even a roommate meetup.

The Two of Cups is about positive emotional connection and expression. What experience is coming forward for you?

Reversal Prompt Questions

How can you remove the block that is keeping you from being compatible with another?

Why are you resisting the needed separation?

How can you release those around you who don't understand or honor your feelings?

Three of Cups

"Let's celebrate one another," proclaims the Three of Cups.

You are meeting the Three of Cups as they gather in a joyful celebration of friendship, reveling in the beauty that is shared connections. The figures hold up their chalices of emotional fulfillment; their clothes of red, orange, and white represent all that is happy, innocent, and passionate. The sky is blue with peaceful clarity as the ground beneath them is fertile and abundant with the rewarding fruits of their labor.

The figures have come together to dance in the joy of connection, success, and creativity. Would you like to join them?

Talking to the Three of Cups in Conversation

When the party arrives, you're invited to grab a glass and join in! The Three of Cups will come forward when you need someone to remind you to celebrate all that is worth celebrating. They are rooted in their collective experience of joyful collaboration, so they may say things like, "When was the last time you let yourself connect with others and celebrate all that has been achieved?" or, "It's time to call your friends and go out!" and even, "How can you join the world around you? What is a community that invites you to be part of it?"

Open to the Three of Cups when you need someone to show you that life is worth celebrating and that there is a community out there waiting for you.

Creating a Personal Connection

When was the last time you connected with your friends? Celebrated with colleagues? Stepped outside of your home and inside of a local community group? Is it coming to mind? Good! Then, you are connecting with the Three of Cups.

They can be found in moments of joy, celebration, and social connection. If you haven't seen the Three of Cups in a while in your own life, I encourage you to connect with them soon. You are worthy of celebration.

Reversal Prompt Questions

What is a block that is keeping you self-isolated?

How can you remove the resistance you feel to allowing yourself to be celebrated?

How can you release the need to overdo it?

Four of Cups

If boredom had a name, it would be the Four of Cups.

You are meeting the Four of Cups here on this grassy hill under a tree of yellow illumination. But as you can see, they are not facing the tree. Instead, they turn their back to it as they look toward three cups they don't seem to enjoy anymore. How can I tell this? Look at the figure's body language. Arms and legs crossed as if completely closing off from what's in front of them. They aren't just closing off from the present options either, but from future ones too. A divine hand attempts to show them a new opportunity, yet the figure cannot see it.

The Four of Cups is the persona of boredom and emotional detachment.

Talking to the Four of Cups in Conversation

When boredom comes calling, I would suggest waking up to the opportunities you are missing out on. The Four of Cups is rooted in their complete lack of interest, so when they come forward, it is with advice such as, "What are you detaching yourself from?" or, "I can see you aren't interested; it might be time to reevaluate," and even, "If this isn't for you that is okay, but don't close yourself off from future opportunities."

Connect with the Four of Cups when you need to see your blind spots to future opportunities and when you need a reminder that detaching from your emotions can lead to detaching from life.

Creating a Personal Connection

Anytime I see the Four of Cups, I am instantly brought back to high school and all the classes I absolutely had no emotional connection to. I was required to take them, obviously, to graduate, but when I was in them, I was just going through the motions, definitely not present at all.

What is an experience in your life where you can remember doing the same? When you were emotionally indifferent and just had zero interest in what was happening?

Reversal Prompt Questions

How can you release the mindset of boredom and get back your enthusiasm?

What is blocking you from accepting new opportunities?

Why is there resistance when it comes to letting others in emotionally?

Five of Cups

With regretful sorrow, the Five of Cups mourns what is lost while hope of the future waits patiently behind them.

As you can see by the figure's black cloak, they are grieving. They carry the weight of their experienced losses literally on their back. The sky is grey, with the only greenery to be seen shown across a bridge the figure is not yet ready to cross. Entranced by their losses, the figure is unable to shift their focus and see the future opportunities awaiting them right at their feet.

The Five of Cups is the persona of not only loss but disappointment and regret. They cry over what has been spilled, even though behind them sits emotional healing and renewal.

Talking to the Five of Cups in Conversation

Sometimes talking with grief helps you heal the grief within you. That is who you will be speaking with when the Five of Cups comes forward: grief. They are rooted in their experience of loss, so their advice will sound like, "Yes, it hurts, but why are you living in this hurt?" or, "I know you are in pain. What actions can you take to begin the healing process?" and, "Do not let the pain of the present lie to you. There is a joy to be found if one were to turn around."

Creating a Personal Connection

Sometimes life hurts, and sometimes it's easier to stay in that hurt than move forward. At least, that is how the Five of Cups feels.

When did you last experience grief? Grief that hurt you so badly you couldn't imagine opening up again. Was it when you lost a loved one or even went through a breakup? Was it when you were denied a job and couldn't see the point in applying to more? These all carry the emotion of loss, and in that experience of despair, you are connecting with the Five of Cups.

I have experienced quite a bit of loss in my life, and that is not me bragging. Those are just the cards I was dealt, and I've come to accept them as they are. But a loss I was not prepared for was the loss of a friend. They didn't pass away, no—that I feel would have brought closure. We simply broke up.

We were friends for over ten years and in each other's lives even longer than that. They were home to me. Our lives were so intertwined that when it ended, I couldn't handle the pain, but I also couldn't handle moving on from it either, because moving on meant it was truly over. After years of healing, I was finally able to reach out for the closure I desperately needed, and I luckily did receive it. We are still not in each other's lives and wish nothing but the best for one another, but the experience will forever be my Five of Cups. It took years, but I was finally able to turn around.

If you are experiencing grief right now, I want to encourage you to turn around. There will be something wonderful waiting for you when you do.

Reversal Prompt Questions

Are you finally ready to release yourself and move on?

What actions can you take to remove the emotional block you have and finally forgive those who have hurt you?

Are you resisting acknowledging the pain you feel because you don't think you can face it?

Six of Cups

Our emotions are not just tied to the present but also to the past. When we go down memory lane, we have a high chance of running into the Six of Cups.

You are meeting the persona of nostalgia and childhood memories, as you can see by the two childlike figures taking time to smell the roses. They are reminiscing in all things nostalgic and comforting. They are in the square of their childhood home, bright with joy and happiness, as their cups of emotional fulfillment bloom with abundance of love. How beautiful it must be to see everything through the eyes of childlike innocence?

They are the embodiment of the childhood memories we hold dear and may even revisit when dreaming.

Talking to the Six of Cups in Conversation

There is nothing wrong with talking to your inner child, especially if they want to remind you of all things joyous. When the Six of Cups comes forward in conversation, they do so to remind you of better days. Their advice will be rooted in their childlike nature and will sound like, "What would little you need at this moment?" or, "How can a lesson from the past help you now in the present?" and, "When was the last time you allowed yourself to openly feel like you did when you were a child?"

It may be difficult to speak with the past, but the Six of Cups is a wonderful persona to call forward when the past can open you up to the future. Bring them forward when you need to use your happy memories to heal the present or when you want to work with the inner child living inside of you.

Creating a Personal Connection

Do you ever look at the past and think, "Wow, those were the good old days." If the answer is yes, you are connected with the energy of the Six of Cups.

You will find the Six of Cups lives in moments located in the past. Moments like looking through childhood photos and remembering how sweet and innocent you were. Or meeting up with a childhood friend and reminiscing about when things weren't so adult.

I know I connect with the Six of Cups every time I talk about my father. He passed away when I was three, and because of this, he lives in the past. Anytime I find myself wanting to connect with him, I look at old photos, listen to my mom and sister share old stories, and even jam out to old music he enjoyed.

But if you find that you are someone who doesn't enjoy revisiting the past, don't worry, you can still connect with the Six of Cups. Every time you go inward and work on healing those emotional wounds, you are sharing a moment with the Six of Cups.

Reversal Prompt Questions

Why are you resisting moving on from the past and living in the present?

How can you remove the hold that your traumatic memories have over you?

What would happen if you were to release yourself from the identity of someone with a traumatic childhood?

Seven of Cups

Not everything is as it seems, and with so many choices, which one is the right one?

You are meeting the persona of illusion and choice paralysis: the Seven of Cups. As you can see, several chalices are in front of the shadow figure, but before you get overwhelmed by all the cups and what's inside, look at the background. These cups are not grounded in reality but are shown in a dreamlike cloud. The background is blue with peace and connection to Spirit, but you cannot see the figure as they have their back to you and are shrouded in darkness, representing that you are meeting them inside of their subconscious. As you look at the cups, you will see symbols of victory, spiritual awakening, material gain, beauty, home, and more. These are all the choices that weigh on the figure, but there are too many options. Which ones do they choose to make a priority and which ones do they walk away from?

Talking to the Seven of Cups in Conversation

When the Seven of Cups comes forward to give advice, understand that the advice is rooted in endless possibilities and that can sometimes feel overwhelming. The Seven of Cups may say things like, "I know you have a lot of options here, but you can't just freeze up. You need to make a choice grounded in reality," or, "Are you daydreaming again about your dream life? How can you take real-world steps to create it instead of just thinking about it?" and, "Not every choice is going to be the right one. Narrow down the one that truly resonates with your core values."

Connect with the Seven of Cups when you need to see all your options. They not only help you see what is available to you but also show you which ones are just there as a distraction.

Creating a Personal Connection

I want you to think about a time when you had so many options that you just sat there and dissociated a little bit.

Was it when you were picking out colleges or planning your wedding? Did you have multiple job offers on the table and were overwhelmed by all the possibilities? The Seven of Cups was present in all these moments. Some large, some small, but all moments when you faced a ton of options and created little fantasies of how they were supposed to turn out.

The last time I connected with the Seven of Cups was when I was creating my brand and had to pick a niche. I mean, how is someone supposed to niche down when people are so multidimensional? The options were so overwhelming, and I found myself looking for any and all distractions to avoid making a choice. Luckily, I was eventually able to choose a cup and find my niche, but that was because I took my time and tuned in to my true feelings.

The Seven of Cups will always appear in moments of indecision and fantasy. Because of this, the best advice I can give you is to stay grounded, evaluate how you feel about each option, and stay realistic about what you can achieve.

Reversal Prompt Questions

How can you remove the resistance you feel to making a decision?

What is blocking you from being realistic about your situation?

What do you need to release to wake up to your reality?

Eight of Cups

The persona of seeking deep fulfillment is here and they are asking you to explore your depths.

You made it just in time to meet the Eight of Cups as they are embarking on what is called a soul's journey. Leaning on a staff of wisdom and guidance, they walk toward a path of yellow illumination. The background is blue with peace while the moon guides the figure deeper and deeper into their subconscious. This will not be an easy journey as you can see. The figure approaches the mountains of challenges and hardships, while a flowing river of emotions sits in the landscape. They are strong enough to overcome these hardships though, as the figure wears a red cape of strength and courage. They are leaving everything behind them. All eight cups of what has been built sit in front of you. The cups are not spilled over or overflowing, they are just there. There is nothing wrong with them. It was just time to go.

The Eight of Cups is the embodiment of walking away from everything. They do not do this in malice but in hopes of returning home to their authentic selves.

Talking to the Eight of Cups in Conversation

Sometimes, you must move on, and that is exactly what the Eight of Cups will advise you to do. They will come forward with advice such as, "Sometimes you have to leave everything behind in order to achieve your dreams," or, "It's time to go within yourself to figure out who you really are," and even, "It's time to walk away from those who don't see you. I know it hurts, but it's time."

Talk to the Eight of Cups when you know it's time to leave but need help figuring out where to go. They will guide you through the dark.

Creating a Personal Connection

I think we can all recall a time when we left or were left. Sometimes leaving is painful. Sometimes leaving is healing. But most of the time leaving is just hard.

When did you have to leave a situation even though doing so hurt those around you? When did you decide to walk away from everything you spent so much time building because it didn't feel authentic to you anymore? Or when did you decide it was time to really focus on yourself and your inner healing, which meant you had to take a step back from everyone else?

If you can resonate with these examples, you are resonating with the Eight of Cups.

Reversal Prompt Questions

What is blocking you from leaving this situation that no longer serves you?

How can you release the mindset that change has to be scary?

Why are you so resistant to taking time for inner healing?

Nine of Cups

Filled to the brim with satisfaction, the Nine of Cups has attained all their emotional and material desires.

You are meeting the persona of personal satisfaction, and believe me, the pleasure is all theirs. As you can see, the figure in front of you is quite pleased with themselves. With a smirk of contentment, they have surrounded themselves with abundance. The background is bright yellow with happiness as nine full cups sit on top of a blue tablecloth. The figure wears a red hat of confidence as they sit proudly in front of their symbols of personal accomplishment.

Talking to the Nine of Cups in Conversation

When the persona of wishes manifested comes forward, you know it's a good sign. Their advice is rooted in how satisfied they are and will sound like, "All you have been dreaming of has finally arrived," or, "Take a moment to allow yourself to feel the emotions that come with being comfortable," and, "Look at how blessed and abundant you are. Enjoy this moment!"

When it comes to finding a path that leads you to total happiness and fulfillment, the Nine of Cups is the persona to help. Bring them forward when you are trying to manifest your dream life and need help tapping into the emotions that will come along with it.

Creating a Personal Connection

It may be difficult to recall an experience when your wishes came true, so let's ground ourselves for a moment and have you remember a time when you just felt emotionally fulfilled. Was it when you were offered your dream job after going through ten interviews that led nowhere? Or maybe when you found out you were having a baby after several rounds of hormone treatments. These are all moments when the Nine of Cups can be seen.

Personally, I find that I run into the Nine of Cups every time I manifest something from my vision board. I know, I know, I am one of those spiritual girlies, but I can't help it! That method of manifestation just works for me, and every time I see something arrive in the physical world that was once created from my inner vision and inner emotions, I am just elated.

When can you recall the feelings of emotional satisfaction? When were you given the experience to indulge?

Reversal Prompt Questions

How can you release your disappointment in how things have turned out for you?

What is blocking you from trusting the universal plan?

Why are you resistant to sharing all that you have in abundance?

Ten of Cups

Happy in all areas of life, the Ten of Cups radiates the energy of total fulfillment. As you can see, this image has a rainbow of all things happy and bright. The sky is a light blue as the landscape shows an abundant and fertile green valley nestling a happy home in the background. The childlike figures play joyously as the parental figures open their hands to praise and thank the universe for providing such blessings.

Talking to the Ten of Cups in Conversation

Who wouldn't want to talk to the embodiment of all things happy and fulfilled? That is who you are talking to when the Ten of Cups steps forward. They are rooted in their happy homelife and healthy relationships, so this is where their advice will always stem from. They will say things like, "Open yourself up to the reality of all things safe and joyful," or, "This isn't a dream, everything really is as good as it seems," and even, "Revel in the bliss right now. You finally have all the happiness you have been searching for."

The Ten of Cups is always the right persona to bring forward when you need to find your rainbow. When you need directions on how to have healthy relationships, emotional fulfillment, and unconditional self-love.

Creating a Personal Connection

Ah, the moments when we sit back and say, "Wow, things really are this good."

The first time I ever met the Ten of Cups in a professional setting was when I was reading for this sweet, shy couple. They didn't tell me why they were getting a reading, just that they happened to be in the area and saw the psychic fair sign. This was a common occurrence, so I did what I always do and performed a simple general reading. At the end, the Ten of Cups popped out, and I told them the happy family they've always wanted is on the way. I mean, it doesn't take a psychic to figure out that when the Ten of Cups lands in the future position, it's a good bet a happy family is in the making. They looked stunned as the wife then revealed to me that they had been undergoing IVF treatments and were about to give up. Now, as an ethical reader, I couldn't guarantee her any sort of future, but I did let her know that a happy, healthy, and fulfilling family was literally in the cards. It was up to them to determine what that looked like.

A few years passed, and I am happy to report that, indeed, the IVF treatments worked, and they have the healthy family they both envisioned. This experience will always be my Ten of Cups.

When can you recall a moment that feels the same? When can you remember feeling not only happy but safe and fulfilled in your relationships?

Reversal Prompt Questions

Why are you resisting opening up to emotional fulfillment? What past traumas are stopping you?

What is blocking you from creating healthy relationships with friends and family?

How can you release the dysfunction in your life?

Page of Cups

An opportunity has arrived to open your heart and connect with your intuitive self. The opportunity's name is the Page of Cups.

Please give a loving welcome to the artist themself, the emotionally sensitive intuitive dreamer of all things imagined, the Page of Cups. You are meeting them right as they gaze directly into the eyes of their subconscious emotions, represented by the blue fish that rises from the chalice in their hand. The page is an emotional figure, as you can see by the blue waves of the sea shown behind them. You can tell the page is a beautiful young and naive soul by looking at their outfit adorned with white water lilies, symbolizing the page's purity, spiritual connection, and fertility.

They are the embodiment of the inner child, and because of this, any messages they bring will invite you to open up emotionally.

Talking to the Page of Cups in Conversation

When the Page of Cups steps forward, they do so with advice rooted in their childlike openness to all things. They ask you to open your heart and mind to all things intuitive, imaginative, and dreamlike. Their advice may sound like, "Do you currently live in your mind or in your body? Can you remember what emotions truly feel like?" or, "When was the last time you shared how you really felt about a situation or person? Now is a great opportunity to do so," and even, "What truths lie within your dreams? What is a message your subconscious is trying to get you to hear?"

Find the sweet Page of Cups when you want to create a life intuitively led. When you need help listening to your heart or healing your inner child.

Creating a Personal Connection

When forming a personal connection with the Page of Cups, I want you to think about a time in your life when you allowed your heart to lead the way. Was it when you started a new relationship and didn't see any red flags or when you tapped into your emotional wellspring and created a beautiful piece of art?

Moments like starting inner child work because you are ready to heal your inner wounds or starting a new dream journal because you know there are intuitive messages trying to swim to the surface. These are all moments of the Page of Cups, but if you can't relate to any, think about the dreamer in your life. Someone who is artistic, thoughtful, and can communicate how they are feeling really well. They make you feel loved and accepted for who you truly are.

If you have someone in mind, take a mental screenshot of that person because they are a great connection to the Page of Cups.

Reversal Prompt Questions

Why are you resistant to connecting with your intuition?

What is blocking you from being creative? Where do you think this block stems from?

How can you release your sensitivity to others' opinions? Why does what they think matter so much to you?

Knight of Cups

The romantic and idealistic lover of the Minor Arcana has just arrived but won't be here long; they have dreams to chase.

You are meeting the Knight of Cups right as they are riding off on their next heart-led adventure. Holding their cup of emotional availability openly toward whoever or whatever comes next. They wear a traditional suit of armor that depicts a redfish of confidence flowing through a stream of intuition. As you can see by looking at the wings placed on their helmet and shoes, the knight is connected to the divine and may even be on a divinely planned mission. The landscape is not lush with abundant love just yet, but you can see the sproutings of green opportunities just across the stream. With a mountain before them, the knight knows a challenge is approaching but does not waver in their quest of desires.

The persona of romantic idealism, the Knight of Cups encourages us to move through life using a heart-centered compass.

Talking to the Knight of Cups in Conversation

When the romantic Knight of Cups rides forward to speak with you, they do so rooted in their inability to do anything that doesn't align with their heart. Because of this, their advice will sound like, "Take a moment to figure out how you feel about this situation or person," or, "How can you invite more romance into your life?" and, "Where is your heart taking you right now? Where are you being called to go from a heart-centered perspective?"

Call on the Knight of Cups when you need to see where your heart is leading you. They can help you see not only the best path to travel but also how it will lead to emotional fulfillment.

Creating a Personal Connection

Have you ever met someone who was just so emotionally available and charming that you fell in love instantly? If someone comes to mind, that person would be a great connection to make with the Knight of Cups, especially if they came attached with a romantic memory, such as a proposal or romantic getaway. Because the knight is, well, a knight, there is movement attachment to them, so when you are making your connection, think of a moment that flowed in and then out.

This can be a romantic proposal, of course, or even the feelings of falling in love, but for a nonromantic connection, think about times in your life when you let your heart do the leading. Such as becoming an emotional support counselor for those in need or even taking the time to connect to your emotional body and allowing yourself to go through the waves of experiencing different emotions.

Connect with the Knight of Cups by connecting with the moments that feel intuitively centered and emotionally vulnerable. What moment is coming up for you?

Reversal Prompt Questions

How can you release the patterns of being emotionally manipulative? Why do you think they developed? What caused them?

What is blocking you from being secure in your emotions?

Why are you resistant to opening yourself up to those around you? Why are you protecting your heart?

Queen of Cups

Empathy and sensitivity make for a great leader. Well, at least according to the Queen of Cups.

Take a moment and look at how beautiful this scene is. The landscape alone has radiating golden hills meeting a gently flowing sea of deep intuition while the sky is a peaceful light blue, inviting you to take a calming breath. Looking at the queen, you can't help but see her holding a majestic chalice of emotional intelligence and spiritual mastery. The queen stares lovingly and tenderly toward the ornate handcrafted chalice. It represents all that she is capable of creating when she does so from a nurturing and heart-centered place. She has mastered these abilities; as you can see, she does not need to touch the water before her. Her emotions do not rule her; she rules them, and because of this, she can use them to nourish the world around her.

The persona of all things caring, intuitive, and emotionally supportive, the Queen of Cups embodies the wisdom of the heart.

Talking to the Queen of Cups in Conversation

Empathy has entered the chat, and her royal highness is ready to listen. When the Queen of Cups shows up to offer her guidance, she does so from a rooted place of love. She has an open heart and supportive arms, so her advice will sound like, "Are you honoring your feelings right now or shaming them?" or, "It's okay to nurture those around you as long as you are doing the same for yourself," and even, "When was the last time you really tapped into your intuition? Can you go to someone who is safe to help you do this?"

Everyone needs guidance every now and again, so bring forward the Queen of Cups when you need someone to show you how you really feel about a situation and how those feelings are valid. The Queen of Cups will not only show you your true feelings but the beautiful life you can create if you were to listen to them.

Creating a Personal Connection

If you have a person in your life who you instinctually go to for advice, you most likely have a connection to the Queen of Cups. The Queen of Cups will show up as figures in our lives who are caring, nonjudgemental, and emotionally validating.

This can be a mother, of course, but it can also be a supportive friend, an understanding spiritual coach, or even your local tarot reader (wink). They are someone who always seems to understand and gives you the best advice in a loving way. When you are with them, you feel safe, seen, and comfortable enough to be emotionally open.

I didn't meet my Queen of Cups until I was thirty-one. I had just started a new job and began to get close to one of the business owners. She was open, kind, emotionally mature, and always tapped into her feelings before deciding, no matter the situation. Kerry and I are now very close friends, but she will always be a model for how fulfilling it can be to lead a life centered around your heart and not your mind.

If you don't have someone in your life you can relate to, that is okay, I promise. Think about a time when you embodied these characteristics. A time when you had to tap into your intuition in order to make a choice or took control of your emotions before they overflowed and possibly created a scene. Every time I use my intuition to lead a decision I make or allow myself the space to express deep emotions, I know I am tapping into the energies of the Queen of Cups.

What are your moments? What or who is your mind recalling right now?

Reversal Prompt Questions

What is blocking you from truly trusting your intuition?

Why are you resistant to speaking openly about your feelings?

How can you release yourself from the pattern of self-sacrifice?

King of Cups

If they are trustworthy, kind, and emotionally available, they are the embodiment of the King of Cups.

You are meeting the king as he sits in comfort upon his throne of stability in the middle of a sea that flows with open emotion. He does not fear being overwhelmed as he is the master of his emotions and knows how to control and channel his feelings in productive ways. He is in balance, holding a chalice of emotional empathy in one hand and a scepter of channeled strength in another. His robes of yellow, blue, and red let you know that he is a joyful, wise, and confident king. He knows that to be a good leader is to be open, compassionate, and intuitive.

The persona of emotional stability, the King of Cups embodies what it means to be responsive instead of reactive.

Talking to the King of Cups in Conversation

The king has arrived to advise, and when he does, it will always be rooted in his emotional maturity. You may hear messages like, "Whose emotional needs are you supporting right now? Yours or someone else's?" or, "How can you find your center during the emotional ups and downs of this situation?" and, "Sometimes you have to look at the situation or person with kindness and love, even if it's difficult."

Bring the king into the conversation when you need to stay calm and channel your feelings toward something productive, not destructive. He can show you how this balance will benefit you on a soul level.

Creating a Personal Connection

When connecting with the King of Cups as an individual in your life, I want you to think of someone who is your emotional rock. Someone who is so emotionally mature that they don't get swept up in situations. Now, this may make you feel as though they are emotionally distant, but that is simply because they know when to open up and lead with their heart and when to shut down and lead with their experience. A person in your life you have been able to count on for nonbiased advice or emotional support when you yourself are overwhelmed. If someone comes to mind, you have found your King of Cups.

If you don't have this type of counsel in your life, think about an experience when you had to be practical and emotionally mature. For me, the King of Cups reminds me of a time when I had to let someone go at my old company. Now, I won't lie, I was the worst King of Cups because I cried the whole time and really didn't want to do it, but nonetheless, I had to detach from my personal emotions about the situation and do my job. It was terrible, and I feel sick just reliving it, but it did create a great personal connection to the energies that make up the King of Cups. In that moment, I was emotionally mature, compassionate, and kind when having to perform my role as a leader.

What is your leader moment when you had to be the same? Is it coming forward? Take a moment and allow yourself to feel it deeply.

Reversal Prompt Questions

How can you release the need to be emotionally manipulative to get what you want?

What is blocking you from sharing how you really feel about this situation? What steps can you take to express your emotions authentically?

Where do you think your resistance to healing your inner wounds stems from? Why aren't you ready to heal?

Chapter Seven

Cementing the Personal Connection

Wow! That was a lot! But you did it! You met all seventy-eight personalities! How do you feel? Do you feel like you were able to form deep connections with each of them, or do you feel a little overwhelmed and need some more guidance?

First, let's take a moment to celebrate what you just accomplished. Digesting seventy-eight different stories is no small feat. You may even feel like you need to rush back and revisit each one to solidify them to memory, but I want you to just wait a moment and take a breath.

Memorization is not the point of this book. I don't want you to feel like you have to remember everything you just read. This mindset can cause you to feel overwhelmed and anxious; I truly don't want that for you.

Instead, I want you to allow yourself to feel proud of what you have already done and then sit in a moment of reflection. Think about what stories really stuck with you. What personal experiences were you able to relate the cards with? If you already have some coming forward, the foundation is setting. That's wonderful!

If you are having trouble, let's go a little deeper and perform an exercise together.

First, what does it take for a personal connection to form? Drawing from my own experience, I think that to form a connection, you have to work on developing and strengthening the skill of empathizing. Empathizing will allow you to step into the shoes of the tarot's personas and see from their perspective.

Need a real-life example?

Let's say you have a friend who comes over and is upset that their childhood pet is sick. When you tune in and empathize with your friend, you can imagine yourself in their position. You might visualize some cherished moments with the pet, like playing with toys, sharing couch cuddles, and maybe even sneaking forbidden table treats. Allow yourself to connect with the emotions that would be present in these moments: joy, happiness, love. Now connect with the emotions that would come forward when realizing the pet is sick and there may be an impending loss.

When you empathize and allow yourself to experience what others are going through, you naturally will connect those feelings to moments you've had in your own life. This then allows you to form your own personal connection, and when something becomes personal, it bonds to us, creating a memorable, impactful, and measurable effect on us.

"I see you because I see myself. I know you because I know myself."

When you apply this experience to reading the tarot, it becomes more than stressful memorization or anxious information recall. It becomes a memory from a moment in time that could be felt within you, seen within your mind's eye and felt within your heart center. This is the power of a personal connection. Taking this power and using it when performing tarot readings opens you up to an entirely new world of intuitive conversations.

How can you practically implement this approach? Let's jump into some hands-on exercises. All you'll need is your tarot deck; a notebook is optional but could be helpful.

Pick up the first card in the Major Arcana, the Fool, and lay it before you. You know the Fool. You've met them before this moment and learned their story. You've taken time to understand their imagery, soaking up the colors of their environment, clothes, and companions.

But now, I want you to put yourself right where they stand.

Take a moment. Imagine yourself standing at the edge of the cliff. What sensations come to life? Can you feel the cold air blowing through you as the sun shines warmly on your face? Or do your ears pick up the sound of your animal companion barking at you, warning you that you are getting too close to the edge? Do your hands feel uneven due to the weight of your stave in one and the weight of the rose in the other? Is your heart beating faster as you get closer and closer to the edge?

Stay here in this moment, and when you're ready, recall a time when you felt exactly like this in your own life. I would hope you haven't actually been standing near the edge of a cliff about to leap into the unknown, but can you recall a time when you had to take a major risk? When did you feel those same sensations as you are feeling now when empathizing with the Fool? What experience required you to be brave, unsure, and maybe even have some blind faith? Was it when you took a risk and asked your crush out on a date? Or when you quit that unfulfilling job with no backup plan whatsoever?

Your connections to the cards don't have to be significant events; they can be, but that isn't a requirement. The only thing they need to be is impactful to you. If they hold meaning in your heart, the cards will hold meaning in your hands.

Let's do another exercise but with a card from the Minor Arcana. Find the Queen of Pentacles in your deck and bring her forward.

The court cards in the tarot seem to be some of the most difficult for people to recall. I even struggled to connect with them, and it's been a fun discussion in my tarot groups because so many of us have shared this experience. But when we employed the conversational method and got to know the court cards personally, it became easier to connect with them.

Looking at the Queen of Pentacles, I want you to again place yourself in her shoes.

Sit on her throne and place your feet in her abundant garden. What is the first thing you notice? Is it the aroma of all the flowers that surround you? The soft footsteps of the rabbit running in front, or is it the weight of the coin you hold as it represents all you have created in this earthly world?

As you sit here, I want you to remember a time when you felt this connected to the world around you. Does a memory of planting a garden come to mind, or maybe even that one time when you were alone on your favorite local trail and were able to connect with the nature around you? Or does the coin's weight remind you how important it was to be responsible with your money because you had to dip into your savings last year for an unexpected family emergency?

These are just a few examples of how the Queen of Pentacles can appear in your own life.

Moving Forward

Now that we have done these exercises together, I encourage you to do this with every single card in the deck. You don't have to do this in one night or make this into a challenge, but if you need to connect to the cards on a deeper, more personal level, this exercise is here to help.

The connections you will make to the tarot will be your own, unique to your point of view and experiences, but that is what will make the cards unforgettable. When you met the cards, they were individuals, and if you take the time to connect with those individuals and empathize with them, well, that is where you will find the magic.

Chapter Eight
Setting Up for Success

Do you ever wish someone would just hand you a manual on how to perform a reading? I certainly did, and that's exactly what I aim to provide you with in this chapter. We'll explore how to read the conversational way and engage in a few exercises we can do together. Believe me, I understand how intimidating reading the tarot can be, so my goal is to help eliminate any confusion you may have and make this whole process more approachable for you.

Performing a tarot reading is an intimate experience that requires you to let down all your walls to open up your energy to the experience. This can make you feel extremely vulnerable, but that's where the beauty of the conversational approach lies. Because once you have formed your personal connections with the cards, those connections should diminish any feelings of exposure when performing readings. You won't be speaking to strangers but friends, confidants, and mentors whom you have already established a level of familiarity with before this moment. The cards have shared themselves with you, so now it is your turn to reciprocate.

To begin, let's first go through some recommended ways to set up for a successful session with your cards.

Setting Up for a Successful Reading

Find a space that works for you, even if it's not a dedicated sacred space. It could be your kitchen table, a cozy corner in your room, or anywhere that feels safe. I performed a reading in a stairwell once, so trust me when I say the cards aren't picky when it comes to where you read them. One thing I do feel is crucial to do when setting up your reading space is cleansing the energy in the area, especially if you're in a shared environment. You can use incense, clearing sprays, or visualization techniques to clear any lingering energies. You want the area to feel lightweight and clean. This will allow you to feel safe and focus on the conversation you are about to begin.

Locking Your Space

After cleansing, I recommend you lock or shield your space. This will allow your conscious self to feel as though the space is protected as well as your energy, creating a confidential environment for you and possibly the person you are reading for. How do you shield your space? Good question! You can use a variety of methods like casting a circle, setting up a grid of protective crystals, or visualizing a bubble of white light in the space. The methods are endless, so find one that resonates with you and makes you feel secure.

Waking Up and Clearing the Deck

After clearing and locking your space, I am sure you are ready to get started, and you are almost there. The next step is to wake up your cards and clear any lingering energy within them. Now, traditionally, this is done by knocking on the deck three times. However, remember there is no right way. You can use your own intuitive rituals of waking up and clearing. In the past, I've used Florida water spray, selenite slabs, and even Reiki breath to wake up and clear my deck, so trust your instincts and do what works for you.

The Shuffle

Shuffling the cards is a personal and unique experience for each reader. There is no one correct way to shuffle. Find a method that feels comfortable for you and your hands. When I first started reading the tarot, shuffling triggered my inner fear of being judged. I didn't want others to see me and think, "Wow, she really doesn't know what she is doing," or come up to me angrily and say, "Silly girl, that isn't the traditional way; you're so embarrassing." Which explains why I was shocked when I shuffled the cards the way that felt right to me, and no one even batted an eye.

You might spread the cards around frantically and gather them back together, divide the deck into two piles and attempt to create the card bridge of your dreams, cut them into three piles as you've seen on TV, or shuffle them repeatedly until the right card flies out. Experiment with different methods and discover what resonates with you. Remember, there is no right or wrong way to shuffle—only the way that works for you.

To Spread or Not to Spread

Tarot spreads are not mandatory in every reading. While they can provide structure and guidance, you have the freedom to choose whether or not you want to use a spread. Traditional spreads like the Celtic Cross or the three-card spread are some fan favorites, but they are not requirements. Some readers prefer a more intuitive approach, asking a question and pulling a single card for guidance. The choice is yours, and if you do choose to use a spread, find one that aligns with your practice, or feel free to create your own.

Pulling the Cards

This may be an unneeded step, but I find a lot of people don't really know how to pull the cards themselves. Whether inside or outside of a spread, they question which way is the right way to pull the cards. You've heard me say it before, and I am sure you will hear me say it again, but there is no right way to pull the cards. Some readers will shuffle the deck once and then pull the cards right from the top. When using a tarot spread, others will shuffle the deck between each prompt and pull the card from the top. I've seen readers spread the deck in a beautiful line as if they are dealers in Vegas and pull the cards that speak to them. My advice is to try all these methods and see which one works best for you. Which method brings you the messages that feel right? You may even have a method outside of the ones listed above, but the point is, just try it all. Keep what resonates and leave what doesn't.

Reading the Conversational Way

All right, the moment has arrived. You've set up your space, prepared your deck, and decided if you're going to use a spread or not. Now, you're ready to begin reading conversationally, but how do you do it?

In the next chapter, I will share with you some beneficial ways of phrasing your questions and even a few tarot spreads that are different topics of conversation, but for now, let's focus on how to read the conversational way. Reading the conversational way means shifting your mindset from just pulling cards and trying to recall their meanings to turning every reading session into a dynamic dialogue between you and the personas of the tarot. This means taking the time to engage with the cards, listen to their advice, reflect on it, and then when you're ready, confidently expand the conversation.

This is why setting your intentions and creating a safe reading environment is so important. I want you to feel comfortable taking your time to have a deep conversation instead of feeling rushed, pulling one card after another, unable to be fully present in the moment. Once you have set your intentions and established your safe space, ask your question and draw a card. Recall who the card's persona shared themselves to be earlier—their personality, story, and voice. Then, deepen the conversation by asking follow-up questions, just as you would in a conversation with your closest friends. Listen to their messages and reflect on how they relate to you.

If something isn't clear, pull another card for clarity, as if asking for more advice on the situation. There is nothing wrong with drawing more cards after you have asked a question. This allows you to weave them into the conversation, taking a moment to see how they connect with each other and build upon the previous messages. Once you feel your first question has been answered, continue the conversation by asking another. This is how you will expand the narrative and open yourself up to talking with multiple personas simultaneously. Trust your intuition and try to remain open to advice that may sometimes challenge you.

I say this because sometimes people fear pulling a bad card such as the Devil, but let me share a little secret with you: *there are no bad cards, just bad readings.* I don't believe the tarot can be defined by such binary terms as good or bad. It is a reflection of our human experience, and sure, sometimes that experience can be brutal, but that doesn't make it innately bad. Removing these labels will allow you to let go of any fear when it comes to pulling the scarier cards of the tarot. When cards like the Devil or the Tower show up in conversation, they do so to bring advice rooted in the harsher moments of life. They invite you to see things from their perspective and recall moments in your life when you have felt just like them.

Think of it like this; when you are talking to a group of friends and asking for their advice, that advice will come from different perspectives because each friend is speaking from different experiences and points of views. This is exactly what happens when you engage in a conversation with the tarot. You wouldn't fear advice from a friend who has had a rougher time than one of your others, right? No way! You love all your friends no matter their backgrounds, so take this love and apply it to all the cards of the tarot. Sure, some may remind you of difficult times or maybe even not have the best intentions in the moment, but we need these perspectives to gain a full understanding of our situation and ourselves.

Putting the Conversational Method into Practice

Now, let's dive into an example where you've already initiated the conversation and are ready to engage in an open dialogue.

A popular one-card pull is often, "How will my day go?" However, this is quite a surface-level question that tends to create an open-and-shut response. You want a response that will spark a conversation. Consider the details when engaging in conversation, whether it's with a person or a deck of energetic cards. The more detailed and focused the question, the better the response.

So, let's rephrase the question. Instead of asking, "How will my day go?" you can ask, "What will my workload be like today at the office?"

You ask the question and receive the Emperor card in the upright position.

You've met this card before, heard his stories, and related them to your own experiences. Hopefully, in this conversation, those memories flood back.

Regardless of the question, the Emperor always offers advice from an authoritative perspective because that is inherent to his nature. It's who he has become because of the experiences he has been through; therefore, it is the lens through which he sees. With this prompt in mind, the Emperor advises you to prepare for a day of hard work at the office. Your efforts will contribute to building a solid foundation for your future. You can apply this foundation to your career, personal life, finances, and more. The work you'll be doing today aligns with your overall structure, so be ready to put on your grinding shoes and, if you feel confident, even take on a leadership role.

How did I arrive at this advice? When I met the Emperor personally and formed a deep connection, I drew upon my own experiences that resonated with his energy. I recalled times when I had to work tirelessly to establish my tarot business, not taking a day off for weeks, or when I had to assert myself and become the leader of my healing journey, no longer relying on mentors for help. These personal connections helped me understand the Emperor on a deeper level.

Now, I invite you to reflect on your own experiences. Can you recall a time when an authoritative figure, like a parent, taught you the importance of discipline by maybe grounding you for getting a speeding ticket, or a time when you had to buckle down and complete a challenging term paper in college, knowing that it would determine your overall grade in the course?

Your parents grounded you so you would take driving seriously and have a solid driving career in the future. You had to buckle down and complete the term paper because if you didn't get a good grade in the course, it would affect your college career. These connections embody the essence of the Emperor—a disciplinary figure and a hardworking leader striving to build a successful foundation.

When you apply these personal connections and present them in a more casual and relatable tone, you'll hear advice like, "Today is going to be a day of strategizing and putting your nose to the grindstone. Make sure to grab that large coffee on your way in; you'll need the energy."

I always want to advise you to take some time to reflect on the card you just pulled before moving on too quickly and pulling another.

We are, of course, going to look at larger spreads as a whole and the overall advice being given, but first, take just a moment and be present with the card in front of you. Connect with its shared experiences, and recall your related memories formed in prior chapters. Sit with this energy, journal the initial advice you feel it's giving, and then move forward.

Expanding the Conversation

Now that we have explored the conversational method through a one-card pull, let's delve into a more extensive exercise.

In this example, we will use a five-card pull to seek guidance on a current situation in your romantic relationship. Initially, working with five cards can feel overwhelming, so we will break down the advice given card by card before examining the overall message.

> **Question One:** What is the current energy surrounding my relationship with my romantic partner?

Card Pulled: The Tower (reversed)

Recalling what you've already learned about reversals, you understand that there may be some resistance present. The Tower represents unstoppable change, like a tornado that cannot be avoided or entirely prepared for. Even the two monarchs on the card couldn't escape the disaster that destroyed their once impenetrable walls.

Interpreting the Advice: If you were conversing with a friend about the situation, you might hear, "You know, you can't avoid the hard conversations forever. Talking about your feelings is important, even if it leads to arguments."

How Did We Get Here: As you become more comfortable with the conversational method, this process will become more intuitive, but by getting to know the persona of the Tower and understanding their experiences, you can interpret the advice in this context.

The cards always offer advice based on their own unique perspectives and experiences. By forming a connection with each card and learning their language, you can understand their meanings and insights, regardless of the question asked. In this case, the Tower's advice reflects their persona as a symbol of unavoidable change.

Question Two: What challenges are my romantic partner and I currently facing in our relationship?

Card Pulled: Seven of Pentacles (upright)

Take a moment to connect with the persona of the Seven of Pentacles. Your mind retrieves the information you learned when you first met this card, similar to recalling details about a new coworker or a recently met friend.

Consider the personal connections you made with this card, and if you have written them down, feel free to revisit those notes. You know they are hardworking and dedicated to their long-term goals. They often offer advice on patience, understanding that the rewards of work take time to manifest.

Interpreting the Advice: The advice from the Seven of Pentacles in this context would be, "Healthy long-term relationships require patience, dedication, and consistent commitment, even when you feel like giving up. Are both of you dedicated to creating and nurturing a healthy partnership?"

How Did We Get Here: As you read the advice and look at the upright Seven of Pentacles, you can see how the advice reflects the persona depicted on the card. This card consistently offers advice related to patience and dedication, regardless of the specific question asked.

Question Three: How can I work through this challenge with my partner to improve our relationship?

Card Pulled: Page of Wands (reversed)

The Page of Wands, your good friend, contributes to the conversation, but in reverse. This can suggest that you might resist following their advice, but it's worth listening to, nonetheless.

Interpreting the Advice: The advice from the reversed Page of Wands is, "Stop procrastinating on having difficult conversations and share your ideas for reigniting the spark in the relationship."

How Did We Get Here: You met the Page of Wands in the upright position as a persona of optimism, fearlessness, and in the beginning stages of their journey. They have all this passion burning inside of them but don't quite know what to do with it.

When pulled in reverse, who they are at their core is being blocked. This is where we get the advice presented above because the upright active energy of the persona is unable to come through.

Question Four: How will working through this challenge strengthen my current relationship with my romantic partner?

Card Pulled: Eight of Wands (upright)

Take a moment and remember that the Eight of Wands embodies speed, freedom, and alignment. Reflect on personal connections you made, such as times when things quickly fell into place or when you expressed yourself freely without hesitation.

Interpreting the Advice: Advice begins to flow: "When you work through this challenge, your relationship will quickly fall back into alignment. Everything will work out just as it should, and you'll move swiftly into the next stage."

How Did We Get Here: The advice aligns with the persona of the Eight of Wands, reflecting their core roots of speed, freedom, and alignment.

Question Five: After connecting with the energy of my current relationship, what guiding advice do you have for me?

Card Pulled: Ace of Cups (upright)

Another figureless card appears, testing your ability to recall the personifications given earlier. Take a moment to reflect and remember your connection with this beautiful overflowing cup representing the unconditional love that overflows onto everything around it.

Recall moments when your cheeks hurt from smiling with friends or when you thought your heart would explode from the love you felt for your first crush. It's an emotion that permeates your entire being, body and soul.

Interpreting the Advice: Due to the nature of the Ace of Cups, especially in the upright position, the advice is centered on love. You may hear advice such as, "No matter the challenge, navigate through it with love," or, "Though this is a challenging time, moving past it will remind you of how your love for each other fills one another's cups." This advice aligns with the persona of the Ace of Cups and, hopefully, the personal connections previously established.

Now that all five cards have been pulled and you have looked at all the advice given by each card persona, I want you to see if you can interpret the overall message. When I look at them all together, the advice I hear is, "Take action and express your needs to create a deeper connection with your partner, even if it is uncomfortable. Once you do this, the relationship will be rekindled, and a renewed emotional connection will be formed fairly quickly."

But I am curious to see what you hear. Take a moment to reflect and journal your interpretation. It's going to take some time to truly understand the conversational method as it not only focuses on your personal connection made with the cards but also taps into your intuition. Because I don't teach you strict meanings and boxed-in interpretations, it can sometimes make you question if that was the right message. That feeling is entirely normal and helpful because it causes you to go back to the personas, reconnect with their stories, and allows your intuition to lead the way rather than your mind.

The best readings are the ones coming from your heart. Where you can look at the cards and, no matter the situation, hear their stories coming through and make connections of your own to those stories. Tarot reading is a practice, so before moving on to the next chapter, where I give you in-depth prompt questions and card spreads, I encourage you to practice pulling one card, two cards, and gradually increasing to five cards.

Greet them, converse with them, and at the end of the day, take the advice that resonates within.

Chapter Nine
Starting the Conversation

Is there anything more awkward than trying to have a conversation with someone but not knowing how to keep the dialogue genuine and meaningful? Even if it's a good friend, sometimes the conversation can just run stale, and you don't really know how to continue. I feel like we have all been there, and when you're talking to a deck of cards, it can be even more difficult to create emotional depth, so let me show you some tried-and-true methods of holding dialogue.

Now, it's important to remember that a good conversation starts with meaningful prompt questions. For example, you wouldn't ask your best friend who just moved, "Hey, all moved in?" Not if you wanted to have a meaningful dialogue with them. That is a question you ask someone if you want to have a quick chitchat while awkwardly waiting for your escape. If you really wanted to connect with them and have an in-depth conversation, you would ask, "Hey, how did the move go? Are you enjoying your new home?"

The same method applies to your deck of friends. You don't want to ask them questions like, "What will my future hold?" I mean, you could, but questions like that would shut down the conversation really quickly once you've received your answer.

Let's set the scene a bit before we get into the type of questions that allow for a deeper and more fulfilling conversation. Picture yourself sitting down for a reading in a place where you won't be disturbed; your favorite warm beverage is next to you, while your newest playlist plays in the background. This moment, this place, just for now, is outside of time. You have nowhere to be, no one to be, and it's just you and your cards.

I set this scene because when you remove the rush of everyday life, you allow yourself to truly open up and let your walls slowly come down. Meaningful questions need to come from a meaningful place. A place where there is no pressure to ask the right questions or automatically know the true meanings of the cards. This place is safe, comfortable, judgement-free, and created just for you and your seventy-eight new best friends who are holding space for you and your inquiries.

Now earlier, when I said meaningful questions, I was referring to questions that begin with *what, when, why, where,* and *how.*

Do you feel like you're back in school learning framework? Good! That is precisely the connection I wanted you to make. You've learned that the tarot speaks to you from their own given experiences and stories, so when you frame your questions in a way that allows their stories to provide you with the answers you seek, it makes the entire process of interpretation so much easier.

Let's do a couple of exercises together.

Prompt Question: How will I know this new job is right for me?

Card Pulled: Six of Wands in the upright position

Interpretation: You've met this celebrity of the tarot before, and you know them as someone whom their peers see as extremely successful. They have achieved their highest goals, and believe me, people are looking up to them. The Six of Wands is here to confirm that this job is the right one for you and that you will know because you will be seen as a winner here. Others will look up to you and celebrate the accomplishments you achieve. It doesn't sound like too bad of a situation to be in.

Now, would you have gotten to the same conclusion if you had just asked, "Is this new job right for me?" Maybe, but a question in that format feels so open and closed. You would have seen the Six of Wands, read it as a yes, and moved on.

How is that meaningful? How is that memorable? It isn't. When you phrase your questions in the "what, when, why, where, and how" format, it allows for an open dialogue to blossom and for a meaningful conversation to take place.

Need more examples? No problem!

Prompt Question: What actions can I take to work through my inner wound of self-sabotage?

You take a breath, center your energy, and pull two cards.

Cards Pulled: The Six of Cups appears in reverse position along with the Chariot in the upright position.

Interpretation: Again, breathing through this, you recall your personal connections formed when meeting these cards. You remember that when a card is pulled in reverse, there is either resistance to the message, a blockage of who the card is at its core, or a release.

Check in with your intuition and ask yourself which reversal interpretation feels right in this context. Is it resistance? Resisting revisiting your childhood and the memories of what your childhood was like? A blockage that prevents you from moving on from your childhood? Or a release of all the trauma that may be residing in your inner child? Which of these reversal interpretations feels right when thinking about the context question of the pull? Even if it's none, I want you to sit here momentarily and allow your intuition to speak.

Once you have found an interpretation that feels right, I want you to move your focus over to the Chariot in the upright position. Recalling your personal connection, I want you to tell yourself out loud how you connected with this Major Arcana card.

Now, use that connection to fit the context of this pull.

For me, when I see the Chariot, I immediately think of movement. But not just any movement: movement with a purpose so forceful that it propels itself forward. It reminds me of when I moved out of my mother's house at eighteen on the day of my high school graduation. I was terrified, but I was so determined to be on my own, nothing was going to stand in my way. I was on a mission of self-discovery, and I wasn't going to stop until I had found myself.

This is my personal connection with the Chariot, and because I have connected it with such an impactful time in my life, it never fails to flow back to me when needing to recall the Chariot's meaning. In fact, it isn't even a conscious effort; it just floods to me immediately. To where, even in this context of the pull question being, "What actions can I take to work through my inner wound of self-sabotage?" I know this action is going to be determined movement.

Now remember, because we have a Major Arcana card and a Minor Arcana card pulled together, the larger influence in the conversation would be the Chariot. Then you have the loving add-on advice of the Six of Cups.

Connecting them from my own point of view would be interpreting the advice as "You need to stop resisting working through your childhood trauma that caused this inner wound of self-sabotage and take real-world steps toward healing."

Doesn't that sound like honest, loving advice you would hear from a friend? Yeah? That is because it is! You are now genuinely engaging in a caring, supportive, and sometimes challenging conversation with friends.

You are conversing with the cards.

Expanding the Conversation with Tarot Spreads

Now, there is more than one way to converse with the cards. A popular way for many is the use of tarot spreads. During our time together so far, I have used one-card pulls, two-card pulls, and five-card pulls, but are numbered-card pulls the same as spreads?

I would say yes, but a tarot spread is defined as pulling the cards in a specific order with different numbered prompt questions *and* placing the cards in a certain shape. When you do a card pull, you typically place the cards in a single line.

Why would a reader use a spread then if they are so similar to numbered-card pulls? Well, although they are alike, tarot spreads offer unique perspectives that can deepen the reading experience overall. A spread can provide insight or clarity on specific issues, bringing structure and depth to the conversation. They can reveal timing or an unfolding story that might be overlooked with just a single-card pull. The reasons are honestly endless, as is the list of tarot spreads.

There are so many popular spreads—such as the Celtic Cross, the zodiac wheel, the pentacle, and the seven-chakra spread—that focus on the exploration of a situation or the self, which I encourage you to explore. Still, due to the nature of this book, I would like to focus on spreads that center around the different topics of conversation. Providing spreads that reflect conversations will allow you to practice the conversational method seamlessly, truly immersing yourself with the cards and strengthening your conversational skills.

Choosing a Signifier Card

Some of the spreads provided will ask you to pull what is called a signifier card or traditionally called a significator card.

What is a signifier card?

A signifier card is a card chosen by the querent when they want to represent themselves during the reading. In my experience, a card is selected, typically a court card, and placed to the side. Court cards are a popular choice because they are associated with people, but since we have turned all the cards of the tarot into people, I want you to experiment with using any card that calls to you.

What card represents you at the moment of the reading? What card represents the energy of the situation you are going through? What card represents the persona you wish to speak to?

Don't like the idea of using a signifier card? That's perfectly fine! Remember, this is your practice, so don't feel obligated to pull a signifier card if it doesn't feel right for you. Your readings will still be meaningful and impactful without one. But if you ever feel you need a little more foundation for your readings, choosing a signifier card may just be exactly what you are looking for.

How Do You Pull Cards When Using a Tarot Spread?

Would you believe me if I told you no one ever taught me this? When I fell into the world of tarot, I was taught a variety of spreads, what they mean, and how they can help you, but never, "Hey, this is how you do it." I know now that is because every reader has their own preferences, so there really isn't a universal way, but I am going to give you some methods I have learned throughout my career. I encourage you to find which one, if any, works for you.

The first way is to have the tarot spread of choice in front of you or in your mind's eye and shuffle the deck while visualizing the spread. Then pull cards from the top of the deck and place them in the spread's shape, trusting that the cards are connected to the spread and will land in the exact positions they are meant to. I like to call this method universal trust because you are truly going with the flow.

The second way starts the same with either having the spread of choice in front of you or visualizing the spread, but this time you are going to shuffle the cards in between each spread prompt question. The difference with this method is for question number one, you would shuffle and then pick the card from the top. Question two, you would shuffle again and then pick the card on the top, and so on. This one still has that universal trust, but in a more directed manner. I like to call this method the Q and A session as you are taking time with each prompt question and consciously sitting with the answers.

Then, we have the method I nicknamed the intuitive ones. This one is where again, you have the spread in your line of sight or your mind's eye, and you simply spread out the entire deck in a row. I've seen readers hover their hands over the cards, selecting all of them at once, and I've seen readers carefully select the cards one by one while viewing the spread. This one, I feel, leans less on universal trust and more on trust in the reader's intuitive senses.

All three are valid methods of pulling the cards for tarot spreads. I have experimented with each and find myself alternating between them based on the spread in use. Additionally, there are other methods not mentioned here, such as shuffling the cards in your hands and letting a card fall out naturally to serve as the answer to the prompt question. But since tarot techniques are unique to each reader, it's impossible to cover all the methods comprehensively.

If all this starts to feel overwhelming, let me offer you a new perspective. Embrace the fluidity and intuitive self-guidance that is inherent when it comes to reading the tarot. This is what I love the most about the practice, and if you can embrace these energies for yourself, they will liberate you instead of stressing you! Through this practice you will discover your true self, finding your confidence and inner guiding light.

Chapter Ten
Conversing through Tarot Spreads

Are you ready to expand the conversation? In this chapter you will explore tarot spreads that were designed to be different topics of conversation, such as love, healing, money, and so on. Each spread will serve as a map, guiding you through layers of questions to hopefully reveal subconscious insights and provide intuitive messages. The shapes of the spreads were designed with three simple intentions in mind: spread topic representation, conversation flow, and conscious focus. I want you to see the imagery of the spread and allow it to speak to the intuitive side of you, but I also want you to be mentally present during the reading. These spreads cover some pretty emotional and possibly triggering topics, so please go into them with self-care knowing that you are safe and speaking with your seventy-eight best friends.

Nice to Meet You Spread

This spread is designed for you to have an introductory conversation with your deck and get to know your cards on a deeper level. What are their likes and dislikes? What are the deck's strengths and challenges? What does the deck intend to teach you, and how can you form a long-lasting relationship?

Card One: What card best represents your personality?

This card will allow your deck to choose a card to represent its energetic personality. Because you have connected with the cards as individuals, it will be nice to see what the overall energy of your deck is. You can keep this in mind when doing readings and form a connection to your deck in a holistic way.

Card Two: What are your favorite topics of discussion?

Asking this question allows for your deck to tell you what topics or areas of your life it would enjoy exploring with you. It allows you to see where this deck can provide the most insight into your life. This doesn't mean it won't be helpful in all areas, but just like we tend to go to certain friends for certain advice, it allows your deck to show off its specialties.

Card Three: What are some challenging subjects for you to give advice on?

Allowing your deck to tell you where it will have challenges allows you both to work through those challenges together. It's like a trust exercise for you and your deck!

Card Four: How can we work through these challenges together?

You and your deck are a team. Asking this question allows you to see how you both can work together to overcome any challenges.

Card Five: What steps can I take to create a deep bond between us?

Allowing your deck to give you real-world steps to take for you both to connect deeper is always a game changer. This deck is one that hopefully will go with you everywhere, grow with you, and become your best friend, so we want you to know exactly what it needs for that relationship to form.

Now that you have had a little meet and greet with your deck, I want to introduce spreads that were created to be different types of conversations. Conversations that you would have with your friends, family, and mentors. Conversations that are informative, emotional, problem-solving, and collaborative, such as love advice, decision-making, career clarity, and so on.

May these spreads guide you to use the conversational method in a way that will bring you confidence, clarity, and healing.

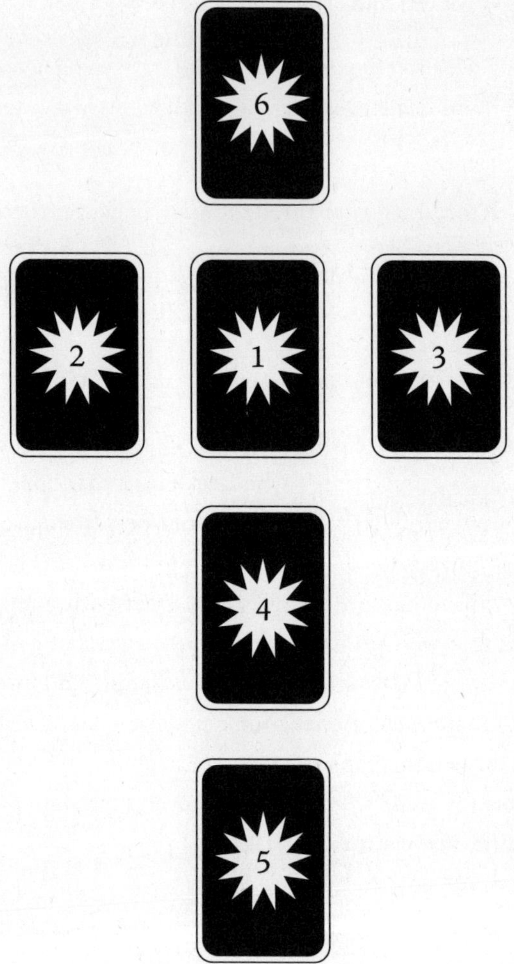

The Decision Cross

If you're like me, you are reaching for your deck of tarot besties anytime you have a decision that needs to be made. Just like you would seek counsel from a loved one, I want you to think of this spread as you going to a trusted friend for some much-needed guidance. This spread is the perfect one to use when you feel as though you're backed into a corner and need your friend to help you see all the angles. You and the cards will talk it out and truly find your best option.

Card One: Choose a signifier card to represent the subject of the decision you are trying to make.

Choosing a signifier card and placing it in the center of the spread will help you tune in to the energies of the situation as well as reveal how you are currently feeling. This is the first step to connecting to your subconscious and bringing it forward.

Card Two: What will the possible outcome be if I choose to make this decision?

The future is fluid and ever changing, but this will allow you to tap into the possible outcome if you were to act and move out of the liminal space that is indecision.

Card Three: What will the possible outcome be if I choose not to make this decision?

This card is there for you to not only see what happens if you were to take no action but to also allow you to see the contrast between the two. That is why both cards two and three are on the sides of the signifier card one. Take a moment to note in your conscious mind the difference between cards two and three.

Card Four: What are the positive energies surrounding the decision?

I am always team to look at the bright side, and normally when you are trying to make a choice there are pros and cons being weighed. Because of this it's important to see what positive energies surround the decision and how they will impact you overall.

Card Five: What are the negative energies surrounding the decision?

As above so below, am I right? When you are seeing the positive it's only fair to look at the negative. The cons may outweigh the pros, so take a minute to tune in to how you feel seeing the two energies in front of you and how they may sway your decision.

Card Six: What action do you recommend I take for my highest good?

I always want the best for you. Always. So will your cards. If you're having a hard time deciding what to do, it's never a bad idea to ask your seventy-eight best friends what choice is ideal for your overall happiness and well-being. Make sure after you pull the final card, you sit in the energy, take in the entire spread, and tune in to how you feel about the overall message. How does the advice make you feel?

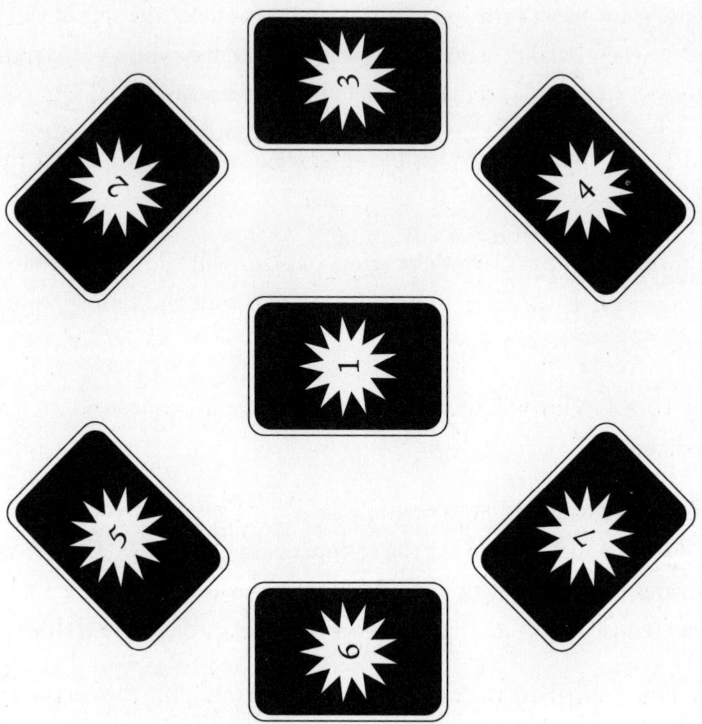

Gaining Clarity on Career

I had to honor my Capricorn rising and put a career spread in this book; it just wouldn't be authentic if I didn't. This spread is all about having a conversation with your cards that centers around how you really feel about your career in the present moment. Just like you would go out with your coworkers and talk about the job, you are going home to your card confidants and getting their advice on how you can find more fulfillment in the career area of your life.

Card One: Choose a signifier card that describes how you currently feel about your career.

As you can see, I love putting signifier cards in the center of a spread when I feel the signifier needs to act as a mirror for the inquirer. When you pull this card and place it right in the center, you put your true feelings about your career into focus.

Card Two: What is a current challenge I am facing when it comes to my career?

When you can see the challenges, you can see what you are capable of overcoming. After you pull this card, make a conscious note of how it made you feel and what advice you are hearing from the persona shown. What was your previous connection to them? What is their personality? What have they been through and are you going through the same?

Card Three: What real-life steps do you recommend I take in order to overcome these challenges?

When you ask for action steps, you are taking the first step to obtaining real-life results from the advice you are being given. This makes the bond with your cards even stronger because they are helping you improve your life here in the material world. Do me a favor and try to follow through with the advice they are giving you. It will make a difference in how you feel overall about your practice.

Card Four: What opportunities are available to me in my current career?

Before you make any drastic decisions, use this prompt to help you see what is available to you where you are right now in your career. After you receive the answer, tune in to your feelings about it. Are you excited, bummed, or apathetic?

Card Five: What opportunities are available to me if do decide to shift careers?

Even though the future is fluid, there is no harm in exploring your options, right? Of course not! See what is out there if you were to broaden your horizons and explore the unknown.

Card Six: When it comes to staying in my current career, what advice do you have?

You've seen your opportunities for staying and for leaving but what is the overall advice if you do choose to stay? I invite you to pull one card or maybe even more if it feels right to you. Pay attention to if the card is from the Minor or Major Arcana. I feel it would make a significant difference for this prompt.

Card Seven: What advice can be given when it comes to leaving my current career?

I think deep down if you are performing this spread and having this talk with your cards about your current career, there is already a little part of you that may have one foot out the door. Don't worry, I am not judging you at all. I am notoriously team "quit your job and follow your fulfillment," so if this spread provides you with the confirmation you need, I am so happy! But if the opposite is true and you are advised that staying in your current career is the best choice for your highest good, I want you to know that it's okay to be disappointed. Connect with this feeling and any others coming forward. Then after you have processed the feelings, see what action steps may be needed for the advice to favor leaving. If that is what you want, of course.

Bravely Relearning to Love

Love, in all its forms, is a powerful force that deeply impacts our lives. Whether it's love for another person, love for oneself, love of an experience or object, we all seek to connect with love's energy. However, finding and sustaining this connection can feel impossible, especially if faced with challenges and past wounds that create fears and blockages. This spread was created to help you bravely recognize and confront these fears, allowing you to work through them using the power of conversation. There is empowerment in facing your fears, and once you are empowered, you allow yourself to be open, connecting back to love in all its forms like self-love, love of others, and love of life. Use this spread to step out of fear and into love-centered openness.

Card One: How do I currently perceive the feeling of love?

Does the energy of love feel distant to you? Painful? Radiating? Or maybe even false? Can you recall feeling love recently at all? Shuffle your cards and see what persona comes forward to be the reflection of your true feelings.

Card Two: What past experiences have shaped my relationship with love?

Experiences influence us; some in positive ways, others in negative. When it comes to the feelings of love, allow your cards to show experiences that made a measurable impact. Were these experiences in the material world as represented by pentacles? Or emotional moments as shown by the suit of cups? What previously formed connections with the personas of the cards are surfacing and helping you connect with the card in this context?

Card Three: How are these past experiences holding me and my personal relationships back?

If these experiences were moments of pain, it's time to revoke their power and stop them from holding you and your relationships back. Use this prompt to see how holding on to the experiences of the past are affecting you here in the present and possibly in the future.

Card Four: What fears do I hold in my heart center when it comes to letting in love?

Fears created by past experiences trick us into building walls to keep us safe. But this is a false security built to keep you trapped in the memory of the past. I encourage you to confront these fears and recognize that they originated in moments that no longer exist. Use this prompt to bring your consciousness to the present and help you bring down those walls.

Card Five: What past event is presently feeding these fears, creating blocks?

Look into the reflection of the painful moment that is continuing to feed your fears around love. A block of fearful protection is being fed and this can manifest emotionally, mentally, or physically. Sit in the feelings that surface and confront the reality of the block's very existence.

Card Six: How can I work through these blocks?

You are deconstructing these blocks and removing their power over you. Be brave and put the steps shown here into practice. Nothing will change if nothing changes, so use this conversation as your starting point and commit to overcoming these blocks that weigh your heart down. Be honest with what you can accomplish and take these steps from a place of self-care and understanding. This is a hard process but one you can do.

Card Seven: When I work through the blocks, how can I improve my personal relationships?

Once you have realigned with the healthy energies of love, how can you use them to positively impact your relationships? Romantic or not, the state of our relationships can serve as reflections of ourselves. Of course, this is not always the case, but if you are in a healthy place with love, it is only logical that you would pour this energy into those closest to you. If you do this, what real-world benefits will you see? That is what this prompt will answer, and I hope it serves as a confirmation that the work you need to do will be rewarded.

Family Ties

Family is a deeply emotional subject, so if you have any significant wounds related to family, please perform this spread when you feel emotionally and mentally safe. Triggers may come forward, and it's important to make sure you're prepared to see them and take the steps needed toward healing. Families are so complex, with cycles passed down through generations, even the best families might create subconscious damage that needs to come toward the surface. This spread is designed to help you see, confront, and heal any wounds created by family dynamics. Whether these situations are happening now or are remnants of the past, use this spread to diminish the hold that pain has on your heart and free yourself from the cycles of family wounds.

Card One: Choose a signifier card that describes how you currently feel about your relationship with your family.

Use this card to see yourself. See how you really feel about your family or your place in the family. You get to choose this card, so take a moment and be as honest as possible. This is your opportunity to say how you feel without any judgement or backlash. Your cards are here to help you; your true feelings are safe here.

Card Two: How am I currently showing up in my family?

Accountability is vital to healing. It can be difficult to process and see, but I want you to be able to view your actions or inactions when it comes to how you are showing up in your family. Remember there are no wrong answers here, no bad cards. Let your cards be the nonbiased friends we all need when asking for advice to help us move forward in the healing process.

Card Three: What are some inner wounds that I have due to my family?

Now is the time to see your wounds. To look at the pains within you and acknowledge their existence. This is the first step, a major step, and I want to tell you how proud of you I am. Pull this card and place it right beside your signifier. How do you feel looking at them together? Do they favor each other or are they opposites? How does seeing your wounds presented in the world feel? Take a moment to process before moving to the next prompt.

Card Four: How can I work through healing these wounds and forgiving my family?

Once you have seen your wounds, processed their existence, it's time to take the next step and get real advice on how to begin the healing process. Sometimes the steps are just seeing the wound's existence, other times it's to voice your pain aloud to diminish its strength. Whatever card comes forward to advise you, if you need to take more steps, feel free to pull more cards and stack them on top of one another as if getting a step-by-step instruction manual. This prompt is not only about healing but also about forgiving. I want you to be able to move forward in your life from a place of healing and not from the perspective of the trauma.

Card Five: How will forgiveness of my family impact my relationship with myself?

Forgiveness is a gift you give to yourself. This pain you have carried from your family has not only impacted your relationship with them but also with yourself. I want you to take all your power back, and one way to do this is to make the conscious decision to free yourself from what your family has done to you. I want you to pull this card and see yourself as whole. You have seen the wounds, seen the healing steps, now allow your cards to show you how forgiveness will impact the way you treat yourself.

Card Six: When I forgive my family, how will it impact my relationship with them?

Now that you have seen how embodying forgiveness will impact you, allow your cards to show you how this choice will affect your family. Remember, you have the power here, so if you choose not to have a relationship with your family, that is your choice, and neither I nor your cards will judge you. But if you want to move forward and be active in your family, this prompt will allow your cards to advise you on how the relationship will be affected.

Card Seven: What overall advice can you give me when it comes to a current situation that I am dealing with in my family life?

I love asking for overall advice because it creates a space for your cards to speak with you freely. They can give you an answer that prompts exploration, consideration, and investigation. Just like in real life where we have friends that all have different opinions on what we should do, this prompt allows your deck of friends to come forward openly about how they think you should handle the situation. You are free to take the advice or leave it, but at least the space to speak is there.

Card Eight: What actions can I take today to follow the advice given?

Speaking of taking or leaving the advice given; I know it's easy to perform a spread, have the conversation, get up from this reading place, and never think about any of this again. I do not want this for you. I want you to receive real action steps you can take after this conversation has ended. This prompt will allow your cards to provide you with those steps, and then the next prompt will encourage you to actually take them.

Card Nine: How will moving forward with the advice given positively impact my overall well-being?

After such an intensive session, I think it's only fair to see how moving forward with the advice given will affect you. There is an incentive here to take real actions because they will yield real-world results. Remember, healing takes time, so don't feel any pressure to take steps immediately, but try to come back to the advice given here when you are ready and see how moving forward with it will bring positive change in your life. I am so proud of you!

Embracing Your Inner Child

Inner child work has such a special place in my heart as I have spent years reconnecting to my own, healing her wounds and helping my clients do the same. I have seen firsthand the blessings that a healed inner child can bring into a person's life, and I want you to experience these blessings as well. The intention of this spread is to provide you with the space to have a conversation with not only your cards but your inner child. Allowing your inner child the opportunity to tell you what it is they need from you to feel safe, seen, heard, and loved. Inner child work can be intense, so make sure you feel ready to have a conversation with little you and hear what they have to say.

Card One: How is my relationship with my inner child currently?

Placed at the very top, this is the present state of your relationship with your inner child. What card is coming forward and how does it feel to see it front and center? Does it bring feelings of closeness or distance?

Card Two: How is my inner child currently feeling?

As you tap into your present self's feelings, open the conversation to go deeper by asking your inner child how they are feeling. Allow them to directly speak with you through the cards and turn the conversation into one of reflection and introspection.

Card Three: What does my inner child need from me to feel safe?

Their needs are your needs. Their pain is your pain. What can you do to meet the needs of your inner child? What persona is coming forward? How does it feel to see them in a context of little you needing what this persona has or needs to have?

Card Four: What action steps can I take to begin nurturing my inner child today?

This card will be your guide to the first steps needed to deepen and strengthen your relationship with your inner child. Nothing wrong with having a healthy relationship with the innocent and sweet side of you, right?

Card Five: What is a message that my inner child wants me to know?

Hand the mic over to your inner child and allow their voice to be the center of attention. This may even be the first time they were allowed this attention, so take a moment and be present in what they have to say. What feelings are surfacing when you reflect on the card pulled? What previous connections are coming forward and how can they relate to your inner child message?

Card Six: How will healing my inner child impact my future self?

Conversations affect us. Sometimes for just a moment, bringing excitement and hope; other times for years with impactful emotions of inspiration and relief. My goal is that this prompt will allow you to see how this conversation could immeasurably impact your future self because your relationship with your inner child has been repaired. See what this process will bring you. What opens for you? How does seeing it in front of you motivate you to take the action steps mentioned above? Reflect on this card and card number one. What does your current relationship look like in comparison with a future one? How does this make you feel?

Integrating Your Shadow Spread

When you step into the world of magic, you venture into the depths of the universe. Here, you explore yourself, freely navigating the deep water of intuition, creation, and death. Within this darkness lives your shadow self, hiding the subconsciously rejected parts of you: trauma, shame, anger, resentment, and unfulfilled desires, just to name a few. Only by acknowledging and embracing these hidden aspects can you truly experience the joy of total self-acceptance. This spread was designed to facilitate an open and accepting dialogue with your shadow self, guiding you toward integration and wholeness.

Card One: Which part of my shadow self is ready to have a conversation?

It takes bravery to come out of hiding. Take time to sit and acknowledge the part of your shadow that has chosen to step forward and speak with you.

Card Two: What life event created this shadow self?

What is their origin story? Just as you met your cards and got to know their stories, what persona is stepping forward now to represent the creation of this shadow aspect? How did you connect with them as a persona and how can you connect with them as a part of yourself?

Card Three: How is this part of my shadow self manifesting in my conscious state?

What lives in the subconscious does not stay there. It finds little ways to rise to the surface. Most of the time it goes unnoticed, but today you are choosing to pull it into your conscious mind and acknowledge its existence. This is a powerful choice and the first step to integration.

Card Four: In what ways am I causing harm to this shadow self?

You are your shadow, and your shadow is you. Anytime you neglect any part of yourself, there will be harm. Use this prompt to see how you are hurting your shadow and how you can repair the damage done. Rejection hurts, but you don't have to live this way anymore. You are stepping into recognition and acceptance!

Card Five: What actions can I take to work through the emotions making me hide this part of myself?

Hiding is easy, and I am sure you could go on hiding these parts of yourself for a very long time because it allows you to avoid vulnerability and rejection, but this is harming you, as you saw with the previous prompt. Be brave and step into authenticity by taking action steps toward freedom of the whole self. See the emotions and take the steps to process them, moving forward along your journey instead of staying stagnant in comfortability.

Card Six: What does my shadow self need from me to come forward and integrate?

This prompt will allow your shadow self to speak with you about their needs. Just like when engaging in a healing conversation with a loved one, you are asking your shadow what you can give to them for them to feel safe, accepted, and therefore safe to come forward.

Card Seven: What blockages or challenges will I need to work through for this integration to be successful?

Integration of the self takes time. There will be challenges that you will need to overcome to be successful, so why not face those challenges head-on? Use this prompt to help you bring any subconscious fears to the surface to overcome them and move forward. This doesn't have to be an unobtainable goal; you can do this and you can trust your cards to help you.

Card Eight: How will this integration benefit me and my relationships?

Relationships make up a huge portion of our lives. Your friendships, romantic partners, family bonds, work relations, and so on. Once you have stepped into the energies of self-acceptance, this is bound to create a ripple effect. Use this prompt to see the real-world benefits of the work you have done here and use it to motivate you to keep going on your self-acceptance journey.

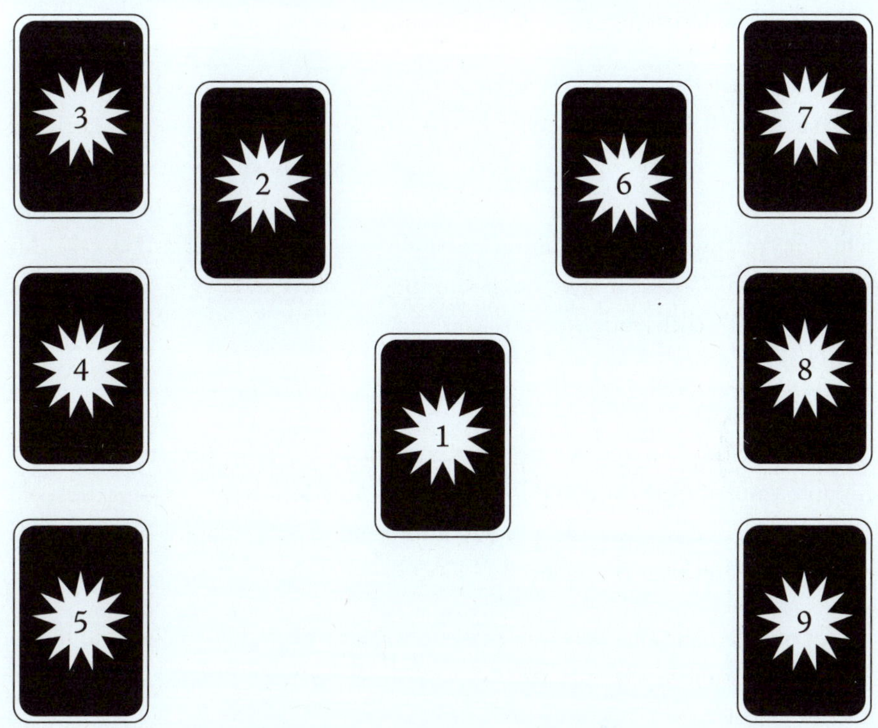

Calling In Limitless Abundance

To end this chapter of spreads dedicated to topics of conversation, I feel it is important that the last conversation center around money. Money often brings forward complex emotions and belief systems that have been in place for generations. Whether you seek to overcome financial fears, attract abundance, or simply cultivate a healthier mindset around wealth, this spread will guide you through an honest conversation with the energies of abundance, bringing you clarity and renewal in your financial well-being.

Card One: What is my current relationship with money?

This is the foundation from which you are going to build the conversation around. You must first be honest with your cards about how you currently feel about money and what the status of your relationship with this energy is. This prompt allows you to see your feelings with your own eyes and have a one-on-one conversation with them. Speak with the card that is placed here and tap into how it makes you feel.

Card Two: What are some of my limiting beliefs that I have around money?

We all have limiting beliefs around money. Some might call it being realistic, but that, in itself, is a limiting belief. Do you think the self-made success stories of the world were realistic with their goals, or did they allow themselves to believe in the possibility of extraordinary abundance? I like to think they embraced a bit of delusion, creating space for limitless possibilities to enter their lives. So, take this opportunity to look at where you are limiting yourself and begin the process of undoing those beliefs with the next prompts.

Card Three: Where do these limiting beliefs stem from?

These beliefs had to come from somewhere, so use this prompt to do a deep dive into your subconscious and root them out. You don't have to accept these old beliefs as your reality and can use this conversation as a stepping stone to heal your relationship with abundance in all its forms.

Card Four: What actions can I take to work through these beliefs and heal my relationship with money?

It's going to take real work, real steps, to undo the past wounds you have centered around money. Take the advice given here and implement it into your real life. What is the first step you can take?

Card Five: How does money energetically feel about me?

This is an important prompt because it allows you to speak directly with the energy of money. Money is not only a three-dimensional piece of paper but also an energetic being. I mean how could it not be? We as humans have assigned it such power and importance it only makes sense that it would take on a life of its own. Speak with money and see with your conscious mind how it feels about you. Once it has spoken, notate how you feel about what was shared.

Card Six: What actions can I take to get closer to money and build a healthy relationship with its energy?

Here is your opportunity to rebuild, reconnect, and realign yourself with the healthiest version of money. Use this spread to take the steps toward building a healthy relationship with the energy of money and see what it brings into your life. What can you and money create together now that you have had an open conversation with one another?

Card Seven: What is blocking money from entering my physical world right now?

There is no shame in wanting abundance to manifest in your physical world as money. I want to make that very clear and remove any shame around this want. Money can bring you security, health, and freedom, so I understand why you would want to discover what blocks are keeping it from being able to reach you. Just make sure you are ready to do the work when it comes to removing these blocks and allowing money to flow freely to you.

Card Eight: How can I work through this block and open myself up to money?

What are the tangible steps you can take? That is what the prompt provides. It's an important question because, just like a financial advisor would send you home with a weekly savings plan, this question allows your cards to give you a real action item to complete. Sometimes the answer will be to let go, as shown by the Hanged Man, and other times, it will be patience with the process provided by the Seven of Pentacles. Either way, you will at least be able to see the answer to what I know can feel like a frustrating situation.

Card Nine: When money flows to me, what do you recommend I do to create a solid foundation where money can continue to grow?

I want you to know the freedom that comes with comfort and security in wealth. This prompt opens the conversation to future planning with money and how you can care for yourself by stopping any patterns of self-sabotage. Your relationship with money is on the mend, and we want to keep it that way.

Chapter Eleven
Practice and Profession

I've referenced having a tarot practice quite often in this book, so I wanted to dedicate this chapter to sharing with you what I define as a tarot practice and how you could turn yours into a professional service that helps others.

What Is a Tarot Practice?

A tarot practice is when you regularly take time to sit down and connect with your cards.

This can look like a daily card pull or a weekly spread reading. This can look like a monthly check-in reading or a biweekly connection session. Every tarot practice looks different, and it's important to remember that a meaningful tarot practice takes time. Connection takes time, so please don't pressure yourself to create one instantly. If you already feel a strong connection and enjoy pulling cards daily, that's wonderful—keep it up! But if you're like me and the idea of a daily tarot practice can sometimes feel overwhelming, I want to ease some of that pressure.

Not everyone thrives on a daily commitment, and that's perfectly okay. Building a consistent tarot practice is about showing up when you can and being gentle with yourself about how often showing up actually occurs. Because when you force yourself to stick to a rigid routine, you are draining the joy right out of the experience.

Some may say that if you don't go all in every day, then you aren't giving it your best. However, in the world of tarot, true enjoyment and meaningful connections arise when you genuinely relish the experience. Approaching the cards out of obligation can strip the practice of its essence and magic. So, let go of any guilt or pressure to practice daily. Instead, find a pace that suits you and brings joy to your tarot journey. Whether you engage with the cards once a day or every few weeks, the key is to be present and savor the moments when you are interacting with your deck.

Your connection with the tarot is a deeply personal one, and it should be tailored to suit you. I want to caution you against falling into the trap of mirroring someone else's tarot practice. In today's online world, it's so easy to feel pressured by what you see and think you're doing something wrong because your practice doesn't look like theirs. But here's the truth: your tarot practice is entirely your own and shouldn't look like another's. Whether you connect with your cards daily, every few days, or even every few months, your practice is valid and meaningful. What matters is that you show up to it when you can and that you do so with authenticity and sincerity.

The takeaway here is to be kind to yourself, okay? Find the rhythm that resonates with you and don't feel bad about it.

Where Do You Start When You Want to Develop a Tarot Practice?

Remember there is no right or wrong way to start your practice; it will vary for everyone. But I will share with you some tips and tricks I've learned along the way, which have helped my clients build their own meaningful practices.

First and foremost, find a tarot deck that truly resonates with you. This step may seem obvious, but it's crucial. Some decks may be visually appealing, but if you don't energetically connect with them, the readings might not feel authentic. You may even receive a tarot deck as a gift, and while you appreciate the gesture, the connection still might not be there; this is also okay.

Building a meaningful tarot practice starts with choosing a deck you energetically love, and finding that deck may take time, but I promise you it is worth the wait. When you connect with your deck, you're connecting with Spirit, forging a powerful bond that will be ever present. Whether you do readings daily, weekly, or even sporadically, that connection will remain alive inside you and your deck. This connection is important, which means you need to take your time and find the deck that speaks to your soul. And sometimes to find that deck, you have to purchase it yourself. I know, I know; I am one of those tarot professionals who believes you can purchase your own tarot deck, and it does not need to be a gift from another.

Because here is the thing: I've bought many decks for myself, and the connection to Spirit is exactly the same as if someone gifted it to me, sometimes even stronger because I was able to feel out the deck's energies in real time. Now let me clarify that I don't underestimate the power of receiving a tarot deck as a gift. When someone gives you a deck from the heart, there's an energetic exchange that happens, leaving a loving imprint that you can feel. This connection creates an instant bond between you and the gifted deck. I completely appreciate and honor the significance of this tradition. It fosters a special bond with your tarot deck and is a beautiful way to connect with both the cards and the person who gave them to you.

However, it's important to recognize and validate that not everyone has personal relationships that lead to receiving tarot decks as gifts. This tradition should never be seen as a roadblock for future tarot readers. Instead, it's a testament to the history and influence of tarot across cultures. So, whether you acquire the deck yourself or receive it as a gift, the bond with the cards is equally potent.

Do You Need Anything Else in Your Practice Other Than Tarot Cards?

Again, each reader has their own preferences, but to be candid with you when starting out, having the right deck is all you need, and even that can be hard to find at first. But if you are curious as to what else you could add to your tarot practice, I am happy to talk about other items that can enhance the experience.

What has always helped me enjoy reaching for my deck on a more frequent basis is that I have a beautiful, sacred space to read them in. I have turned a spare bedroom into a spiritual sanctuary, and that is where my decks live. Decorated with cozy fabrics, spiritual imagery, calming incense, and more, the space calls to me and invites me into it to perform my divination practices.

Now, I understand not everyone is able to turn an entire room into a sacred space. This is where altars come into the picture. An altar is a space where you perform magical workings, and what is more magical than connecting to your inner self or the divine with your tarot cards? Creating an altar doesn't have to be complicated. You can use a shelf, a storage container, or even a drawer—whatever you have, fill it with items that call to you. You can place a beautiful cloth on which to spread your cards, incense for lighting and setting your intentions, or crystals to help magnify, cleanse, or protect the space. Truly, the items are endless.

What Are the Rules of Having a Tarot Practice?

Are there rules when it comes to developing a tarot practice? Personally, I would say no, but the best tarot practice is an ethical tarot practice (in my opinion). But what is an ethical tarot practice? An ethical tarot practice is one rooted in a code of ethics that each reader creates and bases their readings upon.

For example, one of my codes of ethics is that I will not perform a reading for someone without their consent. I will not pull a card for a client regarding an ex-lover or a cranky boss. I require the consent of the person I am reading for. However, this does not mean that readers who do not require consent are not ethical. Every reader will have their own code of ethics that they follow, and some may even have none.

This is why I have been hammering the concept of personal practice throughout this writing. It's important to find what works for you and not judge others on what works for them. You may disagree with how another reads, but I ask you to stay away from labeling others' practices as bad or dark and even good or light. These labels just further create a divide within the communities. I am not saying you have to be friends or agree with how others may read, but I am saying not to discount another's practice just because it looks different from yours.

Are there really no rules when it comes to the tarot? On the surface I would say no—no, there are not. But to add a little nuance, you will find that every tarot reader has their own set of rules, and they may place these upon the readers around them.

To give you a few examples, I've gone over having an ethical practice, and you will find that some readers will have this as a requirement not only for themselves but also for those around them. Some readers will expect new tarot readers to know the history of the tarot and to honor and acknowledge that history. Some readers will expect a new tarot reader to learn the traditional spreads, such as the Celtic Cross, and practice it regularly as if the new reader is part of some sort of apprenticeship. Other readers will expect new readers to take certification courses and learn all the timings of the tarot, all the astrological associations, and so on. The list goes on and on.

To sum it up, no, there technically aren't any rules in tarot itself, but you will find that the readers in your life may have rules. To calm any nerves you may have about these rules, I will share that, in my experience, those rules change per reader and tend to be more of a personal interview than anything else. Every reader has their own personal biases, even me, and those biases come out when you are connecting with those who share the same interests.

This is not to discourage you but to alleviate any pressure you may feel to follow the rules or to make sure you have a good practice. Again, a good practice, if you want to label it as such, is one where you have a deep connection with your cards and can show up authentically. Those are truly the hardest parts of having a tarot practice—forming the personal connections and allowing yourself to show up as yourself. But I know you can do it. Those were two of the main driving points for me writing this book. I wanted to provide you with something that would help you form those connections and provide you with a safe space to show up just as you are, no matter your experience level.

Performing a Reading for Others

Before our time together comes to an end, I want to touch on one of the scariest parts of learning the tarot: reading for others. Becoming a professional tarot reader will not be the end goal for all who pick up this book, but for those who hear the calling and are scared to answer it, I want to provide you with some loving advice.

My advice is simple but will be terrifying to some: *you must start reading for strangers.* When you decide to take the leap, even though you are scared, you will land exactly where you were meant to be. You will never truly be prepared for your first stranger reading. It is impossible to try. What you can do is accept this fact and do the reading anyway. I encourage you to start with those around you who are open to the practice of reading cards. If you do not have any in your personal life, create an online account, advertise that you are just starting out, and let them know you would like to gain some experience. I know this all sounds horrifying, but there are no words to describe the amount of knowledge you will gain from doing this.

When you do take the leap and begin reading for others, I want you to use your voice and remove any fear around asking your clients questions. Ask what has called them to get a reading. Ask them what events are occurring that they need clarity or guidance on. During the reading itself, ask them questions. Does this card resonate with you? Is there a current situation in your life that would explain why this card has appeared? Asking questions is not a crime, and it doesn't make you any less of a professional. As you perform more and more readings, you will find your flow.

I have found that there are three types of professional readers. Those who educate their clients on the meanings of the cards and why that card may be appearing, those who just tell it like it is without any hesitation or worry about how the client will take it, and the ones who rely solely on their intuition to provide messages to the clients.

None of these are better than the others. It depends on who you are and your personality. I myself love to educate my clients and softly walk them through the messages they are receiving, or if I feel my client will be receptive, I will flow into my intuition and do more of a channeling session. But on the opposite end, I love getting readings from other professionals who just tell me how it is and are very blunt with me. This, again, is a personal preference. You will naturally flow into one or the other categories and may even float between them per client. Typically, when I have a client I know doesn't really believe in what I do and doesn't want to be there, I flow into the blunt reader category. I mean, why spend time educating or channeling for someone who doesn't really want to be there?

This is why it's vital for you to read for strangers! When you are exposed to different personalities, you are forced to trust yourself, your relationship with the cards, and your connection to Spirit. You simply stop caring what the client thinks of you because you are answering to a higher calling. You move out of the mindset of, "Oh, I hope that resonated with them," into the air of, "They received the messages they were meant to hear, and I have no control over how they feel about them."

Which is the truth. When you begin your journey as a professional reader, you will have clients who love you, hate you, praise you, bully you, worship you.

This can all feel very overwhelming and triggering, but my advice to you is this: keep reading no matter the client's feelings.

If I had stopped reading the tarot every time I got a client who told me the messages didn't resonate, I wouldn't have been able to meet the clients whose lives I have changed. And those aren't my words; they are theirs. You won't be the reader for everyone. Sometimes you will have clients that fire you, or you fire them. This is entirely normal. You may even receive a bad review that can send you into a shame spiral. But stay grounded in your purpose because if you don't and you quit after that lousy review, you will never be able to receive the ten good reviews that were on their way in the future.

If reading for others is your calling, if it sparks your soul, do it despite the obstacles!

How Do You Give a Reading to Another?

Reading for others is a learned skill, just like reading for yourself. I will tell you that the two can and probably will feel completely different. When you are reading for yourself, you are connecting to not only the personas of the cards but also to your inner self. You are having a conversation with your soul (my opinion), and this instantly brings in feelings of familiarity and ease. When you read for another, your own internal fears can surface and block the messages that were meant to come forward for your client.

So, how can you prevent this from happening? Well, I have found that going into the reading with these three mindsets can help.

Setting Expectations

If you are new or nervous, tell your client this. Trying to be something you are not removes the authenticity from the experience. If you are a new reader, let your client know that so it takes the pressure off you. If you are nervous, tell your client so they can relate to you or provide some words of comfort.

Creating Focus

Focusing on the cards themselves rather than the client is always going to help you get through the reading without your internal dialogue coming up and creating a false narrative of how the experience is going. Focus on the cards' imagery, your connections to them, and how you previously related their meanings to modern-day events.

Embodying Teacher Energy

Teach the client what the cards mean. When I was first starting out, telling the clients who the cards were helped ease my anxiety around looking like a professional. I still do these types of readings to this day because it removes the feeling that I am alone. It allows me to connect not only with the cards themselves but also with the client's spirit team and or higher self. It enables you to embody the energy of an authority figure, which in turn builds your confidence.

For example, when I do this method instead of pulling a card and saying, "You need to take care of yourself," I will say, "This is the Star. The Star is a persona all about freedom of self-expression and having renewed faith. What have you done lately to take care of yourself, and what do you need from Spirit to renew your faith in your current situation?"

This method not only allows me to help my clients form a connection with the cards but also helps them with retention later in the future.

Embodying teacher energy also takes the pressure off you when it comes to how the clients will feel about the reading when they leave. Do you know how many clients I've had look up the meanings of the cards right after a reading? Tons! Do you know what they always say when I have used the teacher embodiment method? "Oh, you were right; this card does mean that!" People are skeptical and distrustful by nature, so if you need to build your own confidence first, try the teacher method in the beginning. Then, you can slowly work your way to becoming more of a blunt or intuitive reader if you so choose.

What Is an Intuitive Reader?

An intuitive reader is a reader who relies on their inner knowing or connection to Spirit to interpret the tarot's meanings. They don't necessarily always give the defined meanings of the cards and instead allow their intuition to flow, providing the messages to the clients.

Is everyone an intuitive reader? Absolutely not, and that's okay. Can anyone be an intuitive reader? One hundred percent!

When I first started reading the tarot, I was not confident enough in my own intuitive abilities to even attempt to channel messages for my clients. It took *years* of personal healing and training to awaken my intuitive self. To channel messages is to release fear of the outcome and doubt within yourself. I had both blocks that I had to work through before I was able to fully embrace the intuitive method.

Only after committing to the inner work can I now tune in or turn on before any reading that I feel would benefit from this type of reading method.

Being an intuitive reader is not a requirement for reading the tarot nor a qualifier of a good or professional tarot reader. I want to make that perfectly clear. The cards themselves are keys to the universal self, so you don't need anything but a connection to them to provide impactful readings for others.

How Can You Become an Intuitive Reader?

I believe that everyone is intuitive and has intuitive abilities. Some of those abilities are stronger than others, but they are there. To become an intuitive reader is to strengthen your connection to yourself and to Spirit. Methods such as inner child healing, meditation, shadow work, self-tarot readings, intuitive strengthening exercises, and so on are a great place to start. Don't let becoming an intuitive reader be your end-all-be-all goal, though. The best readers are readers who accept themselves as they are and show up to help their clients. That is all.

Where Can You Find Clients as a Professional Tarot Reader?

Building a clientele can be a very challenging first step when you begin your journey of becoming a professional reader. I mean how many people actually want a tarot reading, right? So many! Millions of people are looking for guidance and clarity in their lives. The self-help and coaching industry is worth over thirteen billion dollars, which means people are actively searching for help. I say that not in a scammer way but in a way to assure you that your clients are looking for *you*.

So where can you find them? *Advertise, advertise, advertise.*

Advertise locally and globally. When I say advertise locally, I mean start a local online or in-person tarot group, go to your local metaphysical shops, join local psychic fairs, and attend local spiritual events. You must be part of your community to serve your community, and believe me, I know that can be heart-pounding, but remember, you are doing this even if you have to do it scared.

Global advertisement is really my way of saying internet advertisement. Create accounts on multiple social media platforms and build your brand. Tell the world you are open for readings and share with them what makes you different. The clients who are meant for you will find you. Share your personality with the world and let go of the fears that come along with it. You can't help people if you aren't sharing yourself with people.

What Makes a Good Professional Reader?

Remember we are trying to stay away from labels, but if you need a label, in my personal opinion, a good tarot reader is a reader who is authentic and ethical. When I meet another reader and they are truly unapologetically themselves, I fall instantly in love with their energy. Top it off with them being honest, professional, and ethical, well, call me smitten.

A professional tarot reader will share a similar code of honor as do professionals in other fields. They won't lie to their clients. They won't share their client's readings with others. They won't talk about their clients to other clients or anyone else for that matter. They won't pretend to be something they are not.

To become a professional tarot reader is to understand that people need to trust you. You need to become a safe space where people can be vulnerable and feel supported.

To become a professional tarot reader is to become part of something larger than yourself, so please do it with love.

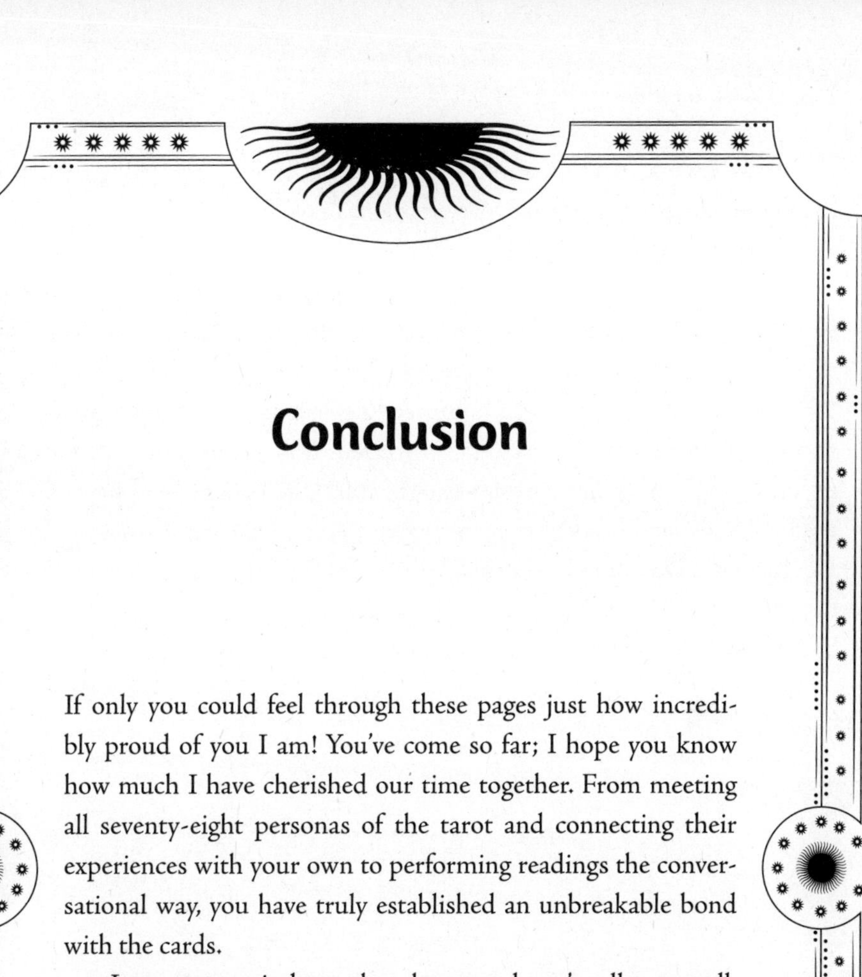

Conclusion

If only you could feel through these pages just how incredibly proud of you I am! You've come so far; I hope you know how much I have cherished our time together. From meeting all seventy-eight personas of the tarot and connecting their experiences with your own to performing readings the conversational way, you have truly established an unbreakable bond with the cards.

I want to remind you that the tarot doesn't call out to all. It calls to those who are meant to hear it, connect with it, and share it. You have heard this call and amplified it within yourself by using the conversational method. This method may not resonate with everyone. For some, it may not feel new or even understandable, but that's okay with me. Those who need it will find it, and that truth sits warmly within my heart.

When I sat down to write this book, it was to create a space where a true soul connection with the cards could be born. A connection so deep that you would not only remember it but feel it. I wanted you to open yourself up to the magic of the tarot and let it transform your life like it did mine.

Now, you may have questions such as, "What about interpreting the cards in different reading scenarios not covered in this book?"

To that, I say remember the point of this book is to help you understand the cards in any given context. That means relying on the foundation of connection you created while reading this book and trusting those connections to translate the messages no matter the questions asked.

The tarot transforms with every reading, as will you. Open yourself up to this transformation and welcome it in without fear or doubt. Sit with the cards in times of joy, happiness, sadness, anger, worry, acceptance, and beyond. Carry them with you and speak to them anywhere and everywhere.

Be brave. Do not hold yourself back for fear of failure or judgement. Expand beyond your self-perceived limits and abilities.

The tarot is limitless in its magic, and so are you.

Bibliography

Adam, Elliot. *Fearless Tarot: How to Give a Positive Reading in Any Situation.* Llewellyn Publications, 2020.

Bright, Steven. *Tarot: Your Personal Guide.* Wellfleet Press, 2018.

Burger, Evelin, and Johannes Fiebig. *Complete Book of Tarot Spreads.* Sterling Publishing, 2011.

Chang, T. Susan. *Tarot Correspondences: Ancient Secrets for Everyday Readers.* Llewellyn Publications, 2018.

Fenton-Smith, Paul. *Advanced Tarot: Discovering Your Inner Wisdom.* Simon & Schuster, 2004.

Fiebig, Johannes, and Evelin Burger. *The Ultimate Guide to the Rider Waite Tarot.* Llewellyn Publications, 2013.

Mantis. *Truly Easy Tarot.* Callisto, illustrated edition, 2020.

Pollack, Rachel. *78 Degrees of Wisdom: A Tarot Journey to Self-Awareness.* Weiser Books, 1980.

Pollack, Rachel. *Tarot Wisdom: Spiritual Teachings and Deeper Meanings.* Llewellyn Publications, 2008.

Wen, Benebell. *Holistic Tarot: An Integrative Approach to Using Tarot for Personal Growth.* North Atlantic Books, 2015.

Wintner, Bakara. *WTF Is Tarot? & How Do I Do It?* Page Street Publishing, 2017.

Acknowledgments

I want to take a moment to acknowledge and thank all the beautiful souls who supported me as I fulfilled what seemed like an impossible dream of writing this book.

Thank you to my husband, whose love and support have never faltered even as I went from a corporate girl boss to a mystical witchy woman.

Thank you to my sister, who has always been my cheerleader and the first in line to support me in all my whimsical endeavors.

Thank you to my mothers, whose love and sacrifices allowed me to grow up in a home where you needn't be anything but yourself.

Thank you to the mystic community, whose open arms welcomed me into a world where I was able to connect with mentors, friends, and clients. I would not be the reader I am today if it hadn't been for your kindness.

Thank you to my friends, who have listened to my anxiety-riddled ravings about this book and have given me nothing but uplifting support.

Thank you to the Sappony people of North Carolina for teaching me to honor my ancestors and showing me how magical it is to have a connection with the land.

Thank you to the divine spirits who honor me with their guidance. I am grateful.

Thank you to the kind and magical people at Llewellyn whose hard work has allowed this dream of mine to become a real-life manifestation.

Lastly, thank you to all the ones who have come before me and paved the way. If it weren't for your voices, I would not have been brave enough to use my own.

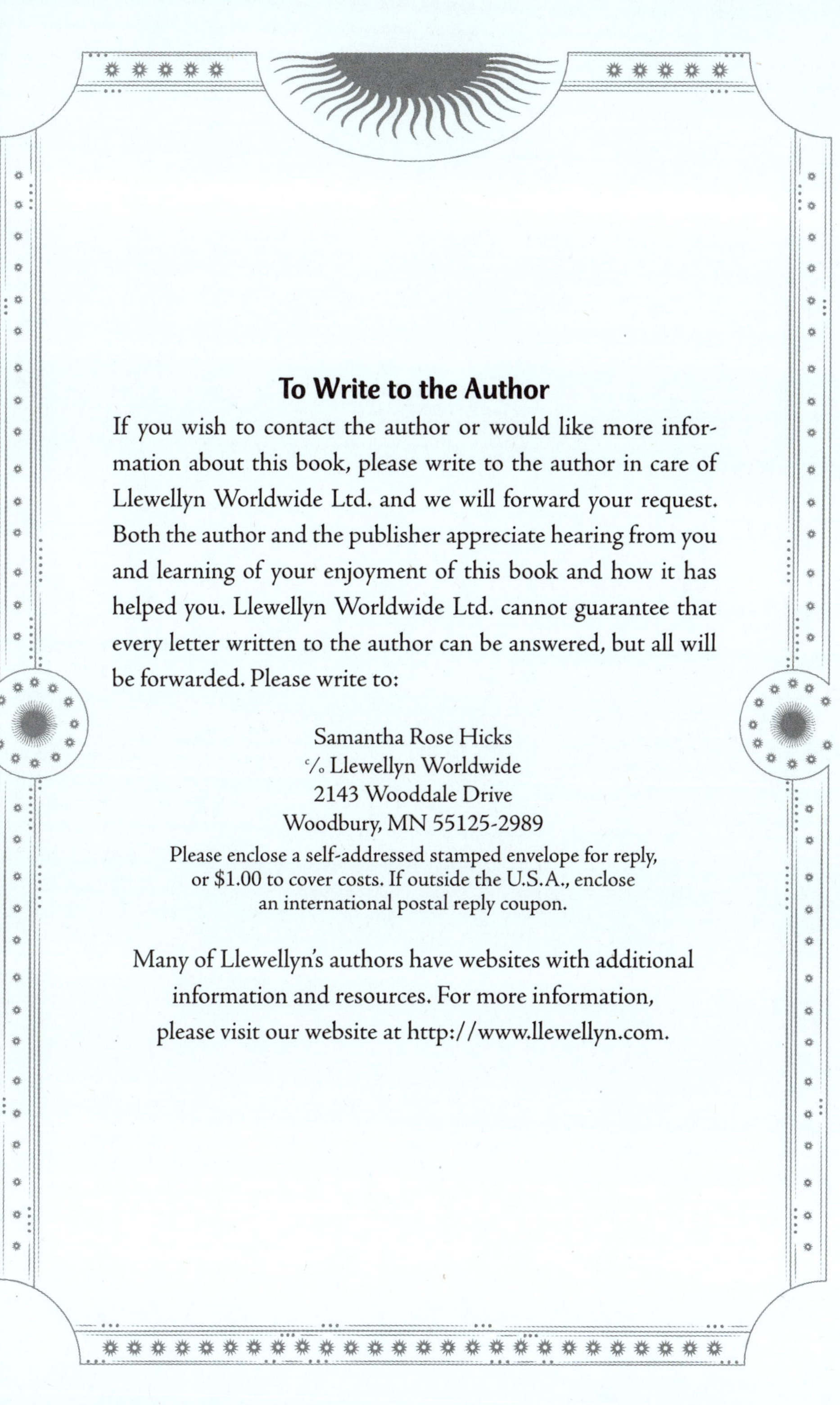

To Write to the Author

If you wish to contact the author or would like more information about this book, please write to the author in care of Llewellyn Worldwide Ltd. and we will forward your request. Both the author and the publisher appreciate hearing from you and learning of your enjoyment of this book and how it has helped you. Llewellyn Worldwide Ltd. cannot guarantee that every letter written to the author can be answered, but all will be forwarded. Please write to:

Samantha Rose Hicks
℅ Llewellyn Worldwide
2143 Wooddale Drive
Woodbury, MN 55125-2989

Please enclose a self-addressed stamped envelope for reply, or $1.00 to cover costs. If outside the U.S.A., enclose an international postal reply coupon.

Many of Llewellyn's authors have websites with additional information and resources. For more information, please visit our website at http://www.llewellyn.com.